LEARNING ABOUT LANGUAGE

D1004174

DISCARDED

Open University Press

English, Language, and Education series

General Editor: Anthony Adams
Lecturer in Education, University of
Cambridge

SELECTED TITLES IN THE SERIES

The Problem with Poetry
Richard Andrews

Writing Development
Roslyn Arnold

Simulations in English Teaching
Paul Bambrough

Writing Policy in Action
Eve Bearne and Cath Farrow

Secondary Worlds
Michael Benton

Thinking Through English
Paddy Creber

Teaching Secondary English
David Curtis

What is English Teaching?
Chris Davies

Developing English
Peter Dougill (ed.)

The Primary Language Book (2nd Edition)
Peter Dougill

Reading Against Racism
Emrys Evans (ed.)

English Teaching and Media Education
Andrew Goodwyn

English at the Core
Peter Griffith

Literary Theory and English Teaching
Peter Griffith

**Lesbian and Gay Issues in the English
Classroom**
Simon Harris

Reading and Response
Mike Hayhoe and Stephen Parker (eds)

Reassessing Language and Literacy
Mike Hayhoe and Stephen Parker (eds)

Who Owns English?
Mike Hayhoe and Stephen Parker (eds)

Language and the English Curriculum
John Keen

Shakespeare in the Classroom
Susan Leach

Developing Readers in the Middle Years
Elaine Millard

Language Awareness for Teachers
Bill Mittins

The Making of English Teachers
Robert Protherough and Judith Atkinson

Young People Reading
Charles Sarland

Learning About Language
Alison Sealey

School Writing
Yanina Sheeran and Douglas Barnes

Playing the Language Game
Valerie Shepherd

Reading Narrative at Literature
Andrew Stibbs

Reading Within and Beyond the Classroom
Dan Taverner

Reading for Real
Barrie Wade (ed.)

Spoken English Illuminated
Andrew Wilkinson, Alan Davies and Deborah
Berrill

LEARNING ABOUT LANGUAGE

Issues for primary teachers

Alison Sealey

Open University Press
Buckingham • Philadelphia

Open University Press
Celtic Court
22 Ballmoor
Buckingham
MK 18 1XW

and
1900 Frost Road, Suite 101
Bristol, PA 19007, USA

First Published 1996

Copyright © Alison Sealey 1996

All rights reserved. Except for the quotation of short passages for the purpose of
criticism and review, no part of this publication may be reproduced, stored in a
retrieval system, or transmitted, in any form or by any means, electronic, mechanical,
photocopying, recording or otherwise, without the prior written permission of the
publisher or a licence from the Copyright Licensing Agency Limited. Details of such
licences (for reprographic reproduction) may be obtained from the Copyright
Licensing Agency Ltd of 90 Tottenham Court Road, London, W1P 9HE.

A catalogue record of this book is available from the British Library

ISBN 0 335 19203 3 (pb)

Library of Congress Cataloging-in-Publication Data
Sealey, Alison.
    Learning about language: issues for primary teachers / Alison
Jean Sealey.
        p.   cm.   (English, language, and education series)
    Includes bibliographical references and index.
    ISBN 0–335–19203–3 (pbk.)
    1. English language—Study and teaching (Elementary).   2. Language
arts (Elementary).   3. Children—Language.   I. Title.   II. Series.
LB1576.S3426   1996
372.6044—dc20   95–23998
                                                          CIP

Typeset by Graphicraft Typesetters Ltd, Hong Kong
Printed in Great Britain by Biddles Ltd, Guildford and King's Lynn

For my mother and in memory of my father

Contents

Acknowledgements

This book draws on work with children, teachers and students in which I have been involved over the past few years. As a primary advisory teacher for the LINC (Language in the National Curriculum) project, I was very fortunate to be able to work with and learn from a number of people, who all brought their own insights and experience to the extensive debate about what children know about language, how they learn and what they should be taught. I should like to acknowledge the contribution to my thinking of all those I encountered through the LINC project, including particularly its director, Ron Carter, who has been most helpful in making available some of the unpublished material which was developed by LINC personnel. I should also like to thank the West Midlands LINC team, coordinated by Leslie Stratta, for the stimulating debates and the ideas which were exchanged. I am very grateful to George Keith for his kind permission not only to adopt but also to adapt for my own purposes the diagram of topics in teaching about language which is included on page 28. The English advisory teachers in Birmingham's Curriculum Support Services also helped to develop my thinking. Various teachers who attended courses connected with the LINC project in Birmingham developed teaching ideas which were disseminated locally, and reference is made to some of these in the text. The multilingual dictionary project referred to on page 108 was developed by Joan Hope of Holte School, working with Stewart Trainor, and the fold-over book project described on page 116 by Irene Barclay of Swanshurst School.

During my time with the LINC project, and also subsequently in my capacity as a lecturer and researcher at the University of Warwick, I have been made welcome in a number of schools, where I have worked alongside teachers and with children to find out more about their knowledge about language. Many of the examples used in the text are taken from these schools and I should like to thank the children who generated the material, and their teachers, particularly in the following primary schools in Birmingham: Deykin Avenue, Foundry Road, Nechells, Osborne, Pegasus, Short Heath, West Heath Infants and West Heath Juniors. Additional examples of children's writing

were supplied by Gail Brigden of Whitmore Park Primary School and Janette
Catton of Eburne Primary School, both in Coventry, and Janet Maybin of the
Open University (who made available some writing by a group of children
with the collective pen name 'Stedmon').

The University of Warwick has provided support in a number of ways. I
received a small grant from the Research and Innovations Fund, which en-
abled me to collect some of the examples of children working with language
which are included in the text. I have also been grateful for a term's study leave
in which to complete the preparation of the manuscript. The University was
also supportive in facilitating the research with a group of students on the BA
(QTS) course who have children of their own and were willing to document
some of the things they said about language. I should like to thank these
students, including particularly Barbara Beardsley, Christine Faulks, Cornelia
Mann, Lynda Maxwell and Angela Vallance, and their children, who are
quoted in the text. Thanks also to my own son, Leon, who has supplied data
of a similar kind and been patient with a mother who has been busily writing
during many evenings and weekends. I should also like to thank Bob Carter for
his practical and moral support.

A number of people have read all or part of the manuscript at various stages,
and I am very grateful for their helpful and insightful comments and suggestions. They include: Tony Adams, Ruth Barton, Bob Carter, Ron Carter,
Urszula Clark, David Hooley, Janet Maybin, George Moore, Leslie Stratta,
Linda Thompson and Sylvia Winchester. I only wish there had been space for
me to develop further the suggestions they made for improvements at various
points. Any errors, omissions and over-simplifications are, of course, my own
responsibility.

General editor's introduction

Alison Sealey's is one of the many books to have emerged at least in part as a consequence of the work of the LINC (Language in the National Curriculum) project directed by Ronald Carter. The history of that project and the unceremonious way in which it was dropped by a government that had very little understanding of what it set out to do has been well documented by now, most notably by Brian Cox in his *The Battle for the English Curriculum* (Hodder and Stoughton, 1995), but in spite of, perhaps because of, the government's attempt to censor its work LINC remains one of the most ambitious and influential incursions into in-service education for teachers of all time.

Alison Sealey worked as a primary advisory teacher on the project and the present volume grows out of her work in that capacity and her own extensive classroom experience. There is a sense in which the work of LINC is today more necessary than ever, given that in all the subject areas of the National Curriculum in England and Wales there is a language requirement built in irrespective of what subject is being taught. Of course, primary school teachers, to whom this book is addressed in the first instance, have always seen themselves as teachers of language throughout the whole curriculum. However, if this is also to be carried through into the secondary school, many teachers will need precisely the kind of help that LINC sought to provide. They will find it in the pages of this book.

This point is made in the hope that the subtitle will not deter secondary teachers of English, and possibly other subjects, from reading it too. Indeed, as under current policies we are likely to see more subject specialism creeping into the primary school, the need for a work such as this, which 'is concerned with children learning about language', becomes more urgent, pointing as it does to the 'opportunities to learn about language wherever learning takes place through the medium of speech and writing'.

Like Alison, I am a teacher educator but my work, unlike hers, is mainly concerned with educating students to be teachers of English in secondary schools. As part of that work I also spend some time with them in primary schools; they often see this as an irrelevance to their main concerns. It is those who feel this most strongly who need primary experience the most. After all children do not spring into being fully formed at the age of transfer from primary to secondary school. What is vital for anyone teaching them at any stage is to understand what the late Andrew Wilkinson called in the title of one of his most influential books, *The Foundations of Language* (my emphasis). As a secondary school English teacher myself at the time when Wilkinson's book was published, I learned a great deal from its pages to inform my own teaching; the importance of early language work and its growth and development was something of a revelation to me at the time. I wish I could have added to its coherent account of theory a book which was, at the same time, strong in terms of practice as well.

While I accept, of course, Alison Sealey's own statement that the complex argument of a book such as this cannot just be summed up in a set of 'bullet points' I think that the reader will find the final pages of the book (when they have read the rest) a valuable continuing source of reference, as will be the glossary which closes the book. For me in the final part of the book the most stimulating section is to be found (beginning on p. 117), dealing with language's 'ludic' (playful) function: 'playing with language, as well as being enjoyable, can be a means of finding out more about its properties and its potential.'

There is sometimes a tendency for books on language to be both abstract and solemn. The present text evades both of these pitfalls. Whilst in no way short of scholarship, research and original thought, the book is also, in common parlance, 'a good read'. Here the wisdom of a university researcher and teacher is linked with the skills and experience of an advisory teacher and, in consequence, the book always has its roots in the classroom. Any experienced teacher will be aware that the same techniques in the classroom can be used at a variety of stages and ages and the practical wisdom in this book can be adopted far beyond the primary classroom that is its main focus. Some of them will certainly be part of my own teaching repertoire with my secondary students in future years.

As I suggested earlier, we are seeing new demands for all teachers to address questions of language in their teaching. A book such as this should make an important contribution to the work of any school planning a series of staff seminars that will enable them to carry out this responsibility in both a humane and responsible manner. It grew out of working with and talking with teachers and students, as the acknowledgements make clear; it speaks on many levels but it will speak especially eloquently to the classroom teachers to whom it is primarily addressed.

Anthony Adams

Introduction

This book is concerned with children learning about language. One aspect of the primary teacher's role is to help children to become increasingly fluent and independent readers, writers and talkers. Primary school teachers also help their pupils to use spoken and written language effectively in all their other learning. These experiences with language are an integral part of children's language curriculum and of their learning about the world, and teachers can draw on them in their teaching *about* language. The approach suggested in this book integrates teaching about language fully into the English curriculum, rather than demarcating it as a separate slot labelled 'grammar' or 'knowledge about language'. It also recognizes that there are opportunities to learn about language wherever learning takes place through the medium of speech or writing.

This is also a book about 'issues', issues raised by three related topics. One of these is what schools are like and what formal education is for. A second is what children are like and how we should think of them as language users and as learners. The third is what language is like and how we should think about it. These may seem to be unproblematic topics, matters of common sense which are familiar to teachers. However, the book suggests that there is not a consensus about any one of them. All of them raise 'issues' because they are controversial, and in the controversies language always plays a key role. The terms in which the issues are debated constitute a vital aspect of the debate itself. So this book, in accordance with the approach it advocates, follows ideas about each of these issues with reference to language, from the language of children's stories to the language of government directives, from the language in press reports about teachers to the language about which young children are puzzled enough to ask questions of their parents and teachers.

The stance taken in the book is that children can learn *about* language by investigating examples of 'naturally occurring' language in use. These examples constitute the 'texts' around which teaching about language is organized. The term 'text' is used here in relation to both spoken and written language, and refers to complete stretches of language in either mode, although in order to form a 'text' suitable for closer study or analysis, speech would usually be transcribed. Texts may be as short as a single word (on a notice, for example) or as long as a whole book. Many kinds of language, with particular functions, can generate the texts from which children can learn about language. This learning may be developed as children produce spoken texts, as they read different kinds of writing, as they gain experience of writing their own texts, and as they use talk to discuss all of these processes. Some examples of the range of texts included at different points in the book to illustrate these potential learning situations are crossword puzzles, children's novels, news-paper articles, radio commercials, casual conversations produced in role play, poems, riddles and dictionaries.

An approach to learning about language which is based on texts has been developing in different areas of language teaching for some time, but it may be unfamiliar to many primary school teachers. I have therefore tried in the book to start from the familiar and to introduce teaching suggestions in contexts which provide some support, especially for readers who lack confidence in their own knowledge about language. Chapter 1, then, reviews some basic ideas about language and introduces the linguistic terminology used in the 1995 version of the English National Curriculum and in later chapters of the book. This chapter takes an approach to the description of language which will be familiar to readers to whom the term 'knowledge about language' means most immediately knowledge of the elements of language, including the dif-ferent categories of words, and how these combine to make sentences. It is a brief review of this approach to linguistic description and readers may wish to follow up the individual topics by reference to other sources.

Chapter 2 presents the idea of language as a social practice, and suggests some implications of this view of language for teaching primary school chil-dren about it. It broadens the perception of language from a collection of elements to a range of 'discourses' which are created and used by people to achieve goals in their lives as social beings. The term 'discourse' is used throughout the book to refer to spoken or written language as it occurs in social and cultural contexts, taking account of the idea that language is a form of social practice, and as such is not neutral or transparent. The texts which I suggest are useful as a source of material for teaching children about language are generated in different social contexts, for different purposes, and the rela-tionships between the people involved in the production and reception of different texts can also vary widely. Social relationships and structures are influential in these variations; thus, as well as a range of specific texts, children encounter a range of discourses which affect their developing understandings about language. Chapter 2 suggests that children are apprentices in the dis-course community in which they are growing up, but they are also active meaning-makers, who contribute to that language and literacy community. The chapter includes examples of children using and learning about language in relation to texts generated in specific social contexts.

Chapter 3 addresses the question of how children's knowledge and understandings about language change and develop as they grow older and progress through the primary school. It takes a critical look at the way in which education policies require us to think about 'development' and what we can assess in children's learning. It also reviews some of the findings available to us from psychological research into children's 'metalinguistic development' – that is, the development of their ability to think consciously and reflectively about language itself. This chapter also attempts to apply the 'microlinguistic' and 'macrolinguistic' knowledge, outlined in Chapters 1 and 2, to the description of primary school children's development, suggesting three dimensions along which teachers might look for and monitor progress in children's learning about language: increasing experience, increasing precision and increasing abstraction.

Chapter 4 takes up the theme that teaching about language is controversial, and explores in more detail why this should be so. It looks at the long-standing tradition of complaining about changes in language, and at the connections between this and the role which education is perceived to play in combating or reinforcing change in people's use of language. The chapter includes a review of milestones in public statements on teaching about language, in the form of the relevant government reports published during this century, exploring the discourses which link national unity with the national language and a national system of education. The final section of this chapter, on standard English, presents the requirements of the 1995 version of the English National Curriculum in the context of a sociolinguistic commentary which explains why these prescriptions are political rather than strictly linguistic.

Chapter 5 attempts to use the primary school itself to demonstrate some of the points made in earlier chapters regarding learning about language from texts. It looks at the range of texts to be found in the typical primary school and offers a commentary on a series of examples, using both microlinguistic and macrolinguistic perspectives to do so. The chapter surveys some of the challenges presented to children, as both readers and writers, by the different kinds of written texts to be found in the primary school curriculum. Various aspects of research into the spoken language of schools and classrooms are reviewed in this chapter, including explorations of two functions of classroom discourse, namely the need for teachers to take responsibility for the socialization, or control, of pupils, and the pedagogical function of talk in the classroom. A section on the discourse of 'child-centred' pedagogy presents some of the conventional contrasts between didactic teaching and 'discovery' approaches, and suggests that it may be possible to develop methods for teaching about language which are not undermined by the disadvantages of the extreme versions of either of these.

The need for some principles to underpin teaching about language is taken up in Chapter 6, which reviews rationales for including learning about language itself as an important component of the curriculum. This chapter suggests some of the conditions which help children in school to learn more about language, including the need for opportunities to 'see' language as a medium, at a conscious level. Various suggestions are put forward about how children may work collaboratively to make explicit their implicit knowledge about language, and how collecting data in the form of texts with authentic purposes and audiences can provide the children with evidence on which to base their hypotheses about language. This chapter also explores how teachers might balance their role as facilitators of children's learning with the need to engage in explicit teaching about language.

Chapter 7 is concerned with specific teaching activities designed to help children learn more about language. The approach which has been developed throughout the book, which places texts at the heart of teaching about language, is exemplified by a range of teaching suggestions, which are presented thematically and include, for example, ideas for composing texts about language and for investigating texts which consist of only one word or short phrases. Among other themes of this kind is the potential of advertisements and poems for teaching various aspects of language, not forgetting some of the ways in which various dimensions of grammar may be approached through actual texts. It is suggested that there are opportunities to teach about language both in the context of language-based projects and also, incidentally, as texts are used in the teaching of other subjects. The chapter concludes with some observations about planning schemes of work and assessing children's achievements in this area of the curriculum.

The conclusion to the book is structured in the form of a checklist of some of the main issues discussed in the other chapters and of the teaching suggestions presented. It is intended as a summary of points which have been raised concerning language as it is deployed in the many texts which are created and encountered by children in school, the tensions between the different versions of schools and of learning with which teachers have to come to terms in many different ways, and the active involvement of children themselves in their learning about language.

1 Knowledge of language, descriptions of language

Introduction

Language is a symbolic system. In order to communicate about things which are not physically present, or which happened in the past, to speculate about what may happen in the future or to handle abstractions of thought or feeling, human beings make use of linguistic signs which stand in for – or signify – components of their experience. The approach taken in this book to teaching primary school children about language will be through the consideration of texts. Texts are the data which form the basis of investigations into language and which generate descriptions of language. As explained in the Introduction, the word 'text' is used in its broadest sense to include stretches of language produced by human beings for genuine communicative purposes, and recorded so that they can be described and analysed. Texts, therefore, may be spoken or written, and we shall encounter quite a large number of texts, and extracts from texts, throughout this book. Descriptions of language are the means by which we account for the way texts are. So for the purposes of deciding what to teach children about language, we begin from an assumption that it is actual texts which we are seeking to describe and account for. This contrasts with an approach to teaching about language which assumes that there are rules about language which were in existence before the texts produced by human beings, and that these have to be learned independently of experiences with actual texts.

This chapter cannot possibly hope to provide a comprehensive description of language, even if it sets its horizon at the level of the sentence. It does seek, however, to introduce the subject of language as a component of the primary English curriculum. Many of the complexities of classification and the different sytems used by different linguists will be simplified in order to do no more than outline briefly the topics relevant for teaching primary school children about language in the context of the revised English National Curriculum. The focus throughout the book is on children learning *about* language, as they learn to use language and as they learn about other things through the medium of language. In this chapter, we shall consider the distinction between implicit and explicit knowledge of language, and we shall look briefly at some of the elements of language which are described in traditional linguistic approaches. The chapter will raise some of the topics covered by linguistic description in relation to the requirements of the 1995 version of the English National Curriculum. Since its focus is on the 'microlinguistic' topics included in the National Curriculum, this chapter should be read in conjunction with the next, where a more 'macrolinguistic' approach is introduced.

Implicit and explicit knowledge of language

Children produce language before they encounter directly or explicitly any of the knowledge about it which has resulted from the description and analysis undertaken by linguists. Children may use different varieties of their first, or 'native', language. In the case of English, for example, they may mark the 'agreement' between subject and verb in the way in which standard English does, as in *he was*, or in the way in which many non-standard dialects do, as in *he were*. Differences like these are the object of some social conflict, which will be explored further in Chapter 4. But both versions can be accounted for within the approach to linguistic description which collects data about what members of a language community actually say and write, and describes the 'rules' of the language accordingly. The vast majority of human beings learn to speak their native language before they begin a formal education in school, which is an indication that children do not need to study language itself in order to make it work for them. There is considerable evidence for language users' implicit knowledge of their own language. Regardless of whether your pupils use *he was* or *he were*, they are very unlikely to come up with a construction like *kit my I home Miss at left games*, rather than *Miss, I left my games kit at home*. In the course of normal communication, language users rarely scramble syntax like this.

An important branch of contemporary linguistic inquiry (following the pioneering work of Noam Chomsky) concerns the initial acquisition of language – how, that is, children come to learn their native language without explicit instruction about what is and what is not a meaningful and well formed utterance. Linked directly with these investigations is the quest for a description of the properties of language which can take account of the basic human ability to learn to use language, no matter which language is involved, in any speech community anywhere in the world. A 'universal grammar' would describe what it is that human beings do when they link units of meaning through words to construct whole utterances. Even a sentence which has never been produced or heard before will nevertheless convey meaning to other language users, thanks to the potential of grammar to combine the separate units of meaning in particular ways. This kind of universal grammar would also account for an innate capacity of the human child to participate in communication through the medium of language.

The details of this kind of linguistic study are not relevant to the main concerns of this book, but they underline the importance of an implicit knowledge of language which children already possess before they start school. Furthermore, many primary school teachers have traditionally discharged their responsibilities for all aspects of the language and literacy work in their classrooms with no background or training in linguistics. Richmond (1990: 27) explains why, particularly for children, an implicit knowledge which is independent of any explicit language study is inevitable:

> The most important kind of knowledge about language is implicit knowledge. Language is such a complex network of meanings and symbols, and the knowledge which users of a language share is so detailed and so vast, that the learning brain, engaged from birth on its enormous task, necessarily operates mainly using the powerful levers of unconscious learning. It could only be that way, for life is not long enough for the conscious acquisition of language to the degree that human beings require and employ it. The gear would be too low, the pace too slow.

This book, however, is concerned with teaching and learning *about* language: we shall consider the explicit knowledge of language which linguists have made available; we shall explore ways in which experiences with texts can help children to make their own implicit knowledge explicit; and we shall look at the role of teaching in extending and developing children's conscious knowledge of language. The history of the requirement to teach children about language as part of the National Curriculum is explored in detail in Chapter 4, but it has its genesis in the Committee of Inquiry chaired by Kingman, whose report also drew a distinction between implicit and explicit knowledge:

> . . . there are different kinds of knowledge. There is the kind of knowledge which people acquire and can act upon, without necessarily being able or needing to explain it: this is 'knowing *how*'. It is what we might call 'implicit' knowledge, as distinct from the kind of knowledge which is analytical, definable, or 'explicit' – knowledge in the sense of 'knowing *about*'.
>
> DES, 1988a, Ch. 5, para. 6, p. 50, original emphasis

The Committee was required to recommend a model of the English language to 'serve as the basis of how teachers are trained to understand how the English language works' and also to specify what 'pupils need to know about how the English language works' (ibid.: 73). Since the publication of its report there have been extensive developments in and modifications to the prescriptions for teaching about language as part of the English National Curriculum. There have, however, been many continuities. One of the features of the model used to describe language which was proposed in the Kingman Report was that it began with the smallest units of language and moved, through the levels, to words, phrases, sentences and finally the structure of discourse. This perspective is consistent with the standard approach taken in descriptive linguistics.

Descriptions of language rely on data, and anyone who wishes to study language needs access to examples of the language actually produced by language users. Written language, of course, is more manageable and durable than spoken examples, and it is only relatively recently that the ability to record, transcribe and analyse spoken language has allowed linguists to recognize the extent of the differences between the spoken and written modes. Whichever is the focus, however, there is a need for a corpus of examples for scholars to use as the basis of study. By reviewing large numbers of examples of naturally occurring language, it is possible to derive hypotheses about patterns that occur in language, such as spelling, syntax, word meaning and so on, and to test these against the evidence of what people say and write. With a quantity of potential material for study which is almost infinite, linguists face the challenge of classifying whatever instances of actual language are to form the basis of inquiry. An obvious starting point is to break up any stretches of language into their constituent parts, and, although this approach begs many questions, some of which we shall return to in the chapters which follow, it is a well established tradition, to be found in many textbooks. Working in this way, language is classified from its smallest units into larger ones, resulting in a hierarchy such as that which was included in the Kingman Report.

The references made to the description of language in successive versions of the English National Curriculum also make use of these levels. It is not that whole texts and the social contexts of language use are completely absent from the study of language which is required, but features of language which are described at and below the level of the sentence occur in each of the three attainment targets. These features are sometimes labelled 'microlinguistic', and they are by no means exhaustive descriptions of language. However, it is useful to be familiar with the knowledge of the microlinguistic elements of texts that is expected and required, and we shall look at each of these in relation to the 1995 version of the English National Curriculum for Key Stages 1 and 2.

Before doing this, I shall summarize the points made so far. There is a distinction between the implicit knowledge of language, which allows children to become fluent speakers of a language without formal instruction, and the explicit knowledge about language, which is the result of conscious reflection and learning. The discipline of linguistics makes available a body of knowledge of the latter type, some aspects of which are prescribed in the English National Curriculum. In order to describe language accurately, linguists make use of the data to be found in texts produced by language users in writing or speech. Traditionally, descriptions of language have been at the 'micro' level, which focuses on sounds, words, phrases and clauses and takes the sentence as the largest unit for analysis. The limitations of this approach will be explored in detail later in the book, but it is nevertheless used as a starting point in this presentation of a text-based approach to teaching about language.

It may be useful at this point to suggest a diagrammatic representation of the relationship between texts and the microlinguistic aspects of language description, although it is important to remember, as Rosen (1988: 10) wrote in response to the enterprise of the Kingman Committee, that 'the history of

Figure 1.1 The 'micro' elements of language

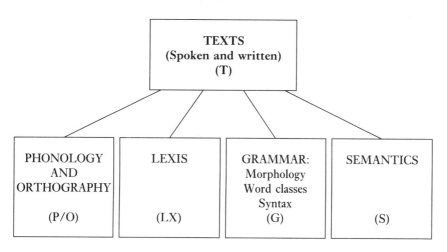

linguistics is littered with attempts to create one definitive model of language,' and that 'language resists being imprisoned in a model'. With that warning in mind, Figure 1.1 is a summary of the topics to be addressed in the remainder of this chapter. The box labelled 'Texts' is there to reinforce the point that, even when, in the study or analysis of language, our attention is on its 'micro' elements, they are to be found in the context of larger stretches of language, which, whether spoken or written, may be thought of as 'texts'. The topics have each been given an initial letter as a shorthand reference, as they will be referred to repeatedly later in the book.

The elements of language prescribed in the English National Curriculum

Phonology and orthography (P/O)

Human beings have access to language partly because they have evolved the ability to produce such a wide range of sounds by using with precision many different parts of the mouth and the complex apparatus involved in breathing. Speakers of a language are able to distinguish, thanks to finely tuned hearing, quite subtle differences between the sounds made as air is passed through and across different arrangements of the tongue, teeth, lips and so on. These abilities are vital in spoken communication, and in writing systems there is a relationship between the sounds of the language and the written representation of it – whether by combining symbols which stand for individual sounds or by means of symbols which denote whole words, since these words are, in their oral form, made up of combinations of sounds. Within the study of language, phonology is concerned with the range and function of sounds in specific languages, while phonetics looks at human sound-making, describing, classifying and transcribing the sounds used in speech. Orthography is concerned with representing the sounds of the language in writing, and for children in primary school this means principally the spelling system of English.

The programmes of study for the 1995 English National Curriculum specify a range of things which children need to learn about phonology and orthography, beginning with an awareness 'of the sounds of spoken language in order to develop phonological awareness' (DFE, 1995: 6). They should encounter texts which include 'language with recognisable repetitive patterns, rhyme and rhythm' (ibid.: 6) and 'use their knowledge of . . . phonological patterns' in their spelling (ibid.: 9). Their phonic knowledge should include being able to recognize 'alliteration, sound patterns and rhyme,' 'initial and final sounds in words' and 'syllables' (ibid.: 7). This phonic knowledge is extended in complexity at Key Stage 2, where there is greater emphasis on orthography. The relationship between the sounds of the language and the symbols used in writing is an important aspect of the knowledge about language specified in the programmes of study. There is reference both to the 'alphabetic nature of writing' and 'sound–symbol relationships' (ibid.: 9) and to 'inconsistencies in phonic patterns' (ibid.: 7). The fact that children are required to build up 'a vocabulary of words recognised and understood automatically and quickly' (ibid.: 7) takes account of the fact that spelling and reading are not associated exclusively with phonic knowledge. Children are required to learn 'common letter strings' (ibid.: 9) and indeed the identification and recognition of *patterns* in sound and print are important aspects of learning about this level of language.

Lexis (LX)

If language is a symbolic system, with symbols made from the sounds human beings can produce and interpret, then it is principally words which are those symbols. 'Lexis' refers to the vocabulary of a language, the words of which it is composed. The programmes of study for the English National Curriculum require children to use an increasingly wide vocabulary, choosing their words with greater conscious attention as they progress through primary school. They are required to develop an 'interest in words' (ibid.: 16) and to play word games (ibid.: 12).

Grammar: morphology, word classes, syntax (G)

Morphology

Like many other languages, although to a lesser extent than some, English makes use of 'building blocks' to combine more than one idea in a single word, and the concept of morphology is helpful in describing how this is done. A 'base' or 'root' word such as *finger* may be made plural by the addition of *-s*.

Finger is a free morpheme, because it can occur freely on its own, whereas the
-*s* is known as a 'bound morpheme', because it is used only in conjunction with
the word to which it is being added to make a plural. The bound morpheme
-*s* also occurs with a word like *walk* when the person walking is a 'third person'
(i.e. not *I* or *you*) and the action is in the present: *She usually walks to work.*
Another bound morpheme which is added to verbs is -*ed*, which indicates that
the action happened in the past: *They opened their presents.* One reason for the
addition of a bound morpheme to a base word is to 'inflect' it. For example, the
suffix -*ed* on *opened* indicates that the action took place in the past, but does not
change the fact that the word has something to do with the action of opening.
Other bound morphemes cause words to change their meaning. For example,
used with words like *happy* or *usual* the prefix *un-* conveys the opposite meaning from that denoted by the base word alone. The English National Curriculum requires children to learn about prefixes and suffixes (ibid.: 7, 9, 16), the
'spelling patterns in verb endings' (ibid.: 7) and 'the spelling of words with
inflectional endings' (ibid.: 16), as well as 'word families' (ibid.: 10, 12) and the
'relationships between root words and derivatives' (ibid.: 7) and 'word structure' (ibid.: 16).

Word classes
The classification of words into categories is specified most extensively in
relation to the teaching of standard English, which is dealt with in Chapter 4.
Some knowledge of word classes is useful for teaching children 'to use the
standard written form of nouns, pronouns, verbs, adjectives, adverbs, prepositions, conjunctions and verb tenses' (ibid.: 16), although it is not clear whether
this terminology is to be taught, nor whether children need to know how to
classify these elements. This aspect of grammar can cause problems, and it
may be helpful to be aware of the different approaches which can be taken to
classifying words (or 'parts of speech'). A familiar approach is to suggest that
words which are nouns can be identified because they name a person, place,
thing, animal or concept, adjectives are descriptive words which qualify and
describe nouns, and verbs are words which express actions, 'doing words', and
so on. Equally familiar are the problems associated with this very limited
approach to the classification of words. It is not only young children who may
find it difficult to identify the 'doing word' as *remembered* in the sentence: *He
remembered the big fight.* And surely *fight* would be a verb in a sentence like:
Fight fire with fire! So what is the difference? A key idea here is that the
classification of words involves a consideration of their function in context
as well as taking account of these very broad generalizations about meaning
(i.e. the notion that a word which is classified as a verb will have a meaning
associated with action).

From a functional point of view, words can initially be divided into two
much broader groups, before concerning students of language (ourselves or
our pupils) with the finer detail of individual classes. Different terms are used
to name these categories, which will be explained below, but the contrast

between the two groups, whichever terms are used, is shown in the two columns:

lexical   grammatical
content   function
open   closed

The first group of words are those which we intuitively recognize as the kinds of 'symbols' referred to above: words which can be made to stand for the idea of some aspect of our experience of the world. Even if there is no concrete thing or property associated with a symbol of this sort, even if the idea it communicates is abstract, like *hope* or *impressive*, there is a symbolic relationship between the word and a concept evoked by it. These, then, are the 'lexical' or 'content' words, and in theory it is possible to go on adding new words to these classes indefinitely, so they belong to an 'open' class of words.

Words in the second group have less work to do as symbolic carriers of meaning, and a bigger role in linking together the ideas conveyed by the first group of words. Their job is more 'grammatical' or 'functional' and new words are rarely added to this group. To illustrate this idea, look at the following two passages taken from a book written for children, both of which have had some of their words deleted. Passage A contains only lexical words (or content words, or those from the 'open' classes) and Passage B contains only those words which belong to the grammatical group (or function words, or those from the 'closed' classes). With so many words missing, you cannot easily make full sense of either passage, but you may be able to make a fair guess at the kind of text you are reading. Which passage is easier to interpret? Why is this?

Passage A
– – – – – time – – – – – – – – – – park – – – – – – – President's house. People let – – – – – horses – – – cows, sheep – – – pigs graze – – – – – park. Today – – – – – – same park – – – – – – – – – – – horses – – cows, sheep – – pigs. – – – – – beautiful park – – – – – – – – – – – – – see.

Passage B
A – was – – – – – to – – – – the – – – –. It was to be – – – – – – – – – – – – – –. – – – – – – – – is an – – – – – – – – – – – – – – that – – – – – 'a – – – – – – – – – – – – –'. – – – – – – – – was – – – – – – – – as a – – – – where the – – – – – – – – – – could – – – – the – – – – of the – – – – – – –.

Adapted from Reading 360, Level 7, Book 4, *The City*, ©
Ginn and Company Limited.

You almost certainly found it easier to guess some of the words missing from A than from B. (The two passages are given in full at the end of the chapter.) The words you lacked in Passage B were all those which carry the 'content' of the text (hence 'content' words as a group), and they are known as belonging to the 'open' classes because it is possible to add new words to these categories as words to label new concepts, experiences or phenomena need to be added to the language. The words you were given in Passage B could be found in almost any text, and they link the substantive ideas together. Rarely does the language need new words to do these 'grammatical' jobs, so they are known as members of the 'closed' classes.

While this approach to classification is not independent of the meaning of individual words, it is also concerned with conceptualizing words according to their grammatical function and distribution in context. You will find that only certain kinds of words occur to you as possible candidates to fill particular slots, and that you are likely to select words from the same class to substitute for a missing word. Attempts to classify words purely in relation to their meaning often do not succeed, and later chapters will explore the implications for teaching children of thinking about the functions of words as well as their meaning.

A third dimension which is available in the process of classifying words is that of form. While this too is far from infallible, many words conform to patterns which indicate which group they are likely to belong to. For example, many words which end in -ly are likely to belong to the class of 'adverbs', words which give additional information about the verb, such as *quickly, happily, impatiently*. Users of English, including children, have an intuitive sense of this pattern, which is demonstrated when they invent adverbs by adding -ly to adjectives. The popular children's story *The BFG* (Dahl, 1982) includes many invented words. The BFG at one point calls Sophie 'a snipsy little winkle'. To gain a sense of what kind of word *snipsy* is, you can substitute other words: what would you suggest? You are highly unlikely to propose words from the closed classes, and the chances are that you will choose an adjective as your alternative. We know that *snipsy* is an adjective even though it is not a word we would find in the dictionary (or in our own personal 'lexicon'), and we know this mainly because of its position in the phrase (after the 'determiner' *a* and before the adjective *little*). The ending -y is another clue, reminding us of other adjectives, like *happy, pretty, naughty*. Now think of one word which would mean *in a snipsy way*, to complete the sentence: *Sophie sat down* ———. What do you think your pupils would suggest?

The knowledge we have of morphology is relevant to thinking about words in this way, as it is often word endings which give us clues about their classification. Thus an -ed ending will often suggest a verb, as, often, will -ing endings. The BFG tells Sophie: 'Please stop higgling me.' What would you say is the base word, or root word, from which *higgling* is formed? Can you make the changes necessary to put it into a sentence about past action, such as the following? *The BFG was annoyed when Sophie* ——— *him*. The kind of words which are hardly ever invented in literature like this (a tradition which includes, of course, the work of Edward Lear and Lewis Carroll) are those which belong to the closed classes, the 'grammatical' words described above. However full of linguistic invention these kinds of stories and poems are, they need to make use of familiar, recognizable words from the 'closed' classes if the reader is to comprehend the text.

These are only some examples of the factors which can help supply clues to word classification, and you can find out more about this in the many textbooks about the subject which would be useful reading to supplement this chapter. (See, for example, Quirk and Greenbaum, 1973; Leech *et al.*, 1982; Thomas, 1993).

Syntax

In addition to some knowledge of morphology and of word classes, the English National Curriculum specifies a limited amount of 'grammatical knowledge', which focuses on 'the way language is ordered and organized into sentences (syntax)' (DFE, 1995: 7), and, at Key Stage 2, involves the development of children's 'understanding of the grammar of complex sentences, including clauses and phrases' (ibid.: 16). In linguistic description, 'phrase' is used to refer to a single element which typically contains more than one word but does not have a subject–predicate structure. A phrase may contain only one word, such as a proper noun or a pronoun, or it may contain several words. This is a sentence from a child's story about smuggling: 'I had my own secret room in the underground caves.' The first word, in subject position, is *I*, and it constitutes a one-word phrase. The predicate, which combines with the subject to make a one-clause sentence, is *had my own secret room in the underground caves*. *My own secret room* is a four-word phrase and the direct object of the verb *had*, and *in the underground caves* is another four-word phrase, this time a prepositional phrase, because its headword is the preposition *in*. Chapter 7 will suggest some strategies for teaching children about this kind of structure in the context of working with complete texts. Complex sentences involve more than one clause, and an important sign of children's developing maturity as writers is their ability to construct a sentence such as *I have a sister who's always doing things wrong* (Burgess *et al.*, 1973: 84), where a less experienced writer might use the simple connective *and*: *I have a sister and she's always doing things wrong*. This aspect of written language is dealt with in greater detail in Chapter 5.

Semantics (S)

The term 'semantics' refers to meanings in language, and, like the other topics addressed in this chapter, it could form the subject of at least a chapter in itself, if not a whole book. However, confining our consideration of the topic to the basic issues which it raises for primary teachers, the English National Curriculum requires children to develop an interest in words and their meanings, including 'their use and interpretation in different contexts' (DFE, 1995: 5). Children are to be encouraged to explore 'words with similar meanings, opposites, and words with more than one meaning' (ibid.: 10). When we encounter a text, one of the strategies we use to make meaning from it is to infer what kind of text it is from the types of word used. For example, if you switch on the radio without knowing the programme schedule, you will use a number of clues to assess rapidly the kind of programme you are hearing. One of these is the 'field' from which words are drawn. So a stretch of talk including the words *taxpayer, interest, rising* and *mortgages* would suggest a news or current affairs programme featuring the domestic economy. The programmes of study require teachers to encourage children to explore 'words associated with specific occasions' (ibid.: 5) and 'groups of words' such as 'the range of words associated with a topic' (ibid.: 12). One of the properties of speech events and written texts of different genres is that, within them, words interrelate and define each other in various ways. The child's story from which a sentence was quoted above contains a range of words associated with the 'semantic field' of its topic, smuggling: *customs duty, unload, goods, boat, smuggler, seas, oceans, caves.* The meaning of some of these words in another context would be different. For example, a story about a servant who was faithful to her mistress might use *duty* in a rather different way, and the meaning evoked by *caves* would be different if the word was read in the context of a textbook about geology.

Further teaching about language required by the English National Curriculum

The topics covered in the foregoing sections give some indication of the teaching about language up to the level of the sentence which is prescribed by the 1995 version of the English National Curriculum. In addition, children are required to learn about the structure and organization of whole texts, and about 'the structure, vocabulary and grammar of standard English' (ibid.: 14). Much of the remainder of this book will address teaching about language which is at the level of whole texts or, where the microlinguistic dimensions reviewed here are encountered, in the context of actual texts. The principles and suggestions for teaching about language which are given in Chapters 6 and 7 will emphasize the importance of a range of text types in children's experience of language, both spoken and written, as a basis for their learning about language from this point of view. Issues which arise from the requirements associated with standard English will be addressed in Chapter 4. One further topic which is included in the programmes of study is children's understanding of 'the similarities and differences between the written and spoken forms' (ibid.: 16), and this is the final topic to be addressed in this section.

Differences between spoken and written language

Like the other topics addressed in this chapter, the differences between spoken and written language cannot be covered in full here, but some basic knowledge is useful in teaching children about language. Many commentators, as we shall see in Chapter 3, believe that the process of learning to read and write is critical for the development of children's awareness of language itself, and, while the two modes of speaking and writing in English share many common linguistic features, there are some differences which are important in any curriculum concerned with the study of language.

If language is a symbolic system, with sounds combining to make words which serve as symbols for aspects of human experience, writing is sometimes described as a second order of symbolism, with written marks used as symbols for the sounds which comprise spoken language. A key difference from a teacher's point of view between the two modes is that while children learn to speak without formal tuition, they do not usually acquire literacy merely by being members of a literate community.

Face-to-face speech incorporates resources which are not found in writing, such as gestures, facial expressions, stress and intonation patterns. (These are referred to as 'paralinguistic' and 'prosodic' resources (see glossary).) Writing has its own systems for indicating the relative importance of different aspects of a text, the placing of pauses, and so on. Learning to write involves learning these systems, such as layout and punctuation, in order to make the transition from speech required for writing. Children also need to learn how to compensate for the absence of an 'interlocutor', or partner in dialogue, as writing typically involves greater distance than speech, in space and time, between the producer and the receiver of language. The programmes of study require opportunities for children to 'read their work aloud in order to understand the connections between the punctuation of a sentence and intonation and emphasis' (ibid.: 9), and they are expected to learn the finer details of punctuation as they become more expert with the written mode of the language.

The differences between spoken and written language are not confined to the microlinguistic elements. Because it is written language whose lexis and grammar have been most easily analysed, with spoken language proving much more difficult to pin down and describe, and also because of the microlinguistic tradition which focuses on units no larger than the sentence, it is only relatively recently that some important aspects of the two modes have become apparent. Written language and spoken language may perform a similar range of broad functions (Nunan, 1993), but the contexts in which the respective modes are used are likely to be different. Typically, speech is more dependent on context than writing. The clauses in written texts tend to be syntactically more complex, and to contain a higher ratio of lexical (or content) words to grammatical (or function) words than is true of speech (Halliday, 1989). Speech often 'chains' ideas together using simple clause patterns with little subordination and is associated with an informal style in many contexts. However, the two modes are not absolutely distinct, and, on a continuum of formality, for instance, a conventional lecture (which may actually be written language read aloud) is likely to be nearer the most formal end, while a note passed between students in the audience (who *are* co-present in space and time) may be more informal and elliptical.

When people are talking spontaneously, composing their utterances on the spot, as it were, it is quite usual for them to repeat themselves, interrupt each other, pause to think but continue to 'hold the floor' by saying *um* or *er* while

they formulate the next part of their contribution. Minor syntactical inconsistencies are typically tolerated among people speaking, because they do not
interfere with understanding. These features of speech have led some commentators to regard it as an inferior form, and writing gains prestige because
it can be carefully 'crafted'. However, far more speech than writing is generated around the world each day, and if we want to know what language is like,
we need to study its spoken as well as its written form. The different qualities
of the spoken language have implications for any attempt to prescribe a 'standard' version of the language. The very process of codifying a language into a
written system tends to 'standardize' it, which leaves lots of questions remaining about what might be meant by 'spoken standard English'. This is a matter
of social values and attitudes, and the topic of speech/writing differences
therefore bridges the concerns of the present chapter and the next, which
moves beyond the elements of language.

Using microlinguistic knowledge in the context of a text

It will become clear in the rest of this book, and particularly in the next
chapter, that microlinguistic descriptions such as those briefly outlined here
are inadequate as a guide for teachers teaching primary school children about
language. However, microlinguistic knowledge is useful for many experiences
involving language, and any text may be thought of in part as constructed out
of the elements of the language. To illustrate some children's microlinguistic
knowledge in action, I have chosen a crossword puzzle as the text to explore,
and I shall relate it to Figure 1.1 (p. 5), using the letters given in the diagram
as references to the areas of linguistic knowledge used by the children. Crossword puzzles are an interesting genre of text, in that they bridge the receptive
and productive relationship. In other words, like questionnaires, they require
one to be both a *reader* of the text as it is presented and a *writer* of the text as
the clues are solved and the answers entered on to the grid. I shall suggest later
in the book that teaching children about language may be successfully integrated into other language work, not necessarily under the headings of 'Speaking and Listening', 'Reading' and 'Writing', but in contexts where children can
move between the language modes.

Because the text to be written consists of single words (LX), the crossword
puzzle allows the solver to concentrate on a microlinguistic challenge, without
reference to phrases, clauses or sentences (G). Nevertheless, there are some
generic conventions of the text as whole which the reader/writer needs to
know before engaging with it (T). The layout of the grid is of critical importance, and it is necessary to understand which part of the grid is referred to by
each of the clues. These are set out in a way which assumes that the reader will
know, without detailed instructions, what has to be done to fit the word into
the right place when the clue is solved, and that the number given in paren-
theses after each clue indicates the number of letters in the answer.

The example I shall quote here is of two girls, Marcia and Saleema, tackling a published crossword before composing their own as one part of a longer text they were writing: along with other children in their Year 4 class, they made a Christmas annual, a book of puzzles and stories for some younger children in their school. The crossword they looked at had the theme of a haunted house, which immediately narrowed the semantic field from which they would expect to draw when trying to find the answers to the clues. So, probably unconsciously, the children used their semantic knowledge (S), in association with their knowledge of the vocabulary of the language, their lexical knowledge (LX), to approach the task of solving the puzzle. Some of the words were found almost immediately and written into the grid, although to do this they had to draw on their knowledge of orthography (P/O), and spelling mistakes delayed them. Their intuitive knowledge of word classes meant that in every case they looked for and suggested words which were from an appropriate class (G), although this was not made explicit. Like most crosswords, the words needed were from the 'content' or 'open' classes (in this case mostly nouns), and when they made their own puzzles later they chose such words too.

The clue with which they had the greatest difficulty was: 'unpleasant mixture made in a cauldron (4)'. Two letters were written in, thanks to clues solved already, so they needed to complete 'B-E-' to finish the crossword. Their strategies moved between the semantic, trying to find a synonym (S), and the phonic/orthographic, trying to find a combination of letters which would generate a suitable word (P/O). At one stage, on the advice of the teacher, they used their alphabetic knowledge to eliminate impossible combinations. This is an extract from the discussion:

Teacher: What letter could fit before that *E*?
Marcia: I.
Teacher: Could be. What else? Go through the alphabet. Could it be *BAE* . . . ?
Marcia: Yes! *BEAT*.

Saleema realized that *BAET* was not the correct spelling of *BEAT*.

Saleema (pointing): That's supposed to be *E* and that's supposed to be *A*.
Teacher (to Marcia, confirming this): Could be, but it isn't. It would be the wrong way round if it was *BEAT*. Could it be *B*? Could it be *B-B* something?
Saleema: No.
Teacher: Why not?
Marcia: BB.
Saleema (laughing): Because nothing begins with a *B-B*.
Teacher: Could it be *B-C* something?
Saleema & Marcia: No.
Teacher: Why not?
Saleema: Nothing begins *B-C*.
Teacher: OK. Go through the letters, and see if you can think of a letter that it could be.

The two girls started to do this, listing the letters of the alphabet on a space on the page and putting a tick or a cross to indicate whether the combination was possible. They carried on until they reached *B-I*, and invented a word *BIET*, to rhyme with *DIET*. Eventually, re-reading the clue, Saleema suddenly thought of *BREW*, and exclaimed 'Brew, brew, a witch's brew!'

Saleema was using her implicit knowledge of 'collocation' – words which are likely to occur together in texts – when she put the word *brew* into this phrase. *Brew* could occur in a passage about beer-making or a story about having a cup of tea, but in the context of a 'haunted house' crossword, remembering this phrase was a helpful piece of semantic awareness.

Primary school children's experience is saturated with instances of the need to utilize their unconscious knowledge of the micro aspects of language such as those demonstrated in this brief encounter with a specific text. This knowledge can be made explicit by the need to articulate it. For example, Saleema had already internalized the conventions of English sound and spelling systems sufficiently to be able to state confidently that 'nothing begins with a *B-B*'; indeed the very idea made her laugh. The teacher could have taken the opportunity to extend this partial knowledge of possible letter combinations by getting her to research, from written texts in her reading repertoire, more about this aspect of sounds and letters. For example *B-B* is not an impossible combination: consider *rubber* or *nibble*. So what is the difference? Children could investigate this, as they might Marcia's suggestion of *baet*: do any words use this combination of vowels? What sound does it represent? It would be possible to build up a classroom display of the findings, consolidating for the children who did the research and for their classmates some of the knowledge about 'common letter strings' required by the English National Curriculum. The semantic and grammatical knowledge deployed in the completion of this text could also be made explicit. The children decided to give their own Christmas annual the theme of 'creatures', and this was reflected in the texts generated. The words they chose for their own crossword puzzles and word-search puzzles were more predictable because they came from a particular semantic field and from the open classes of words. This work was an experience of language which added to knowledge that was mainly implicit. The implicit knowledge, though, would be available to be made explicit, and extended, at a later date.

Conclusion

This chapter has introduced the idea of teaching children about language as an integral part of the language work with texts which they will be carrying out to meet the requirements of the programmes of study for speaking and listening, reading and writing. It has drawn a distinction between the implicit knowledge about language, which all language users possess as part of their ability to communicate, and the explicit knowledge, which is the product of conscious reflection and explicit teaching. A brief review has been presented of what we have called the 'micro' elements of knowledge about language required by the 1995 version of the English National Curriculum, relating these to Figure 1.1, which emphasizes texts as the data from which any students of language, including children at school, learn about the properties of language. Finally, we have looked at the microlinguistic knowledge which was used, made explicit and extended in the context of classroom work with a specific text.

I want to conclude this chapter by reiterating the difficulties associated with trying to produce too rigid a model or classificatory system with which to try to encapsulate language, which is not a rigid, neat or static entity. Again, my example is taken from the Christmas annual project described above. Another child, Hilary, decided to produce a different kind of language puzzle for the book, based on two lists of paired words, each presented in a different order. The object of the puzzle was to look at each word in the first list and then find its pair in the second list. So *thin* had to be matched with *fat*, *hot* with *cold*, and so on. These examples all involved opposites, but Hilary also included *cup* in one list and *saucer* in the other. This led to an explicit discussion of how words can be grouped in pairs, and what the exact meaning of *opposite* is. She decided to produce two puzzles, one of 'pairs' and one of 'opposites'. In her original lists she had included *boys* and *girls*. The discussion between the children about which puzzle these words should be in and whether *boys* and *girls* are pairs or opposites was lively and never resolved. The children had encountered a fundamental problem in classifying language. It can sometimes be impossible to determine the meanings of words without reference to social context. It is the social dimensions of language which are the subject of the next chapter.

The full text of the passages which appeared earlier in this chapter, with some words deleted, to exemplify the difference between content and function words is as follows:

Passage A
At that time there was a park near the President's house. People let their horses and cows, sheep and pigs graze in the park. Today in that same park there are no horses or cows, sheep or pigs. It is a beautiful park for everyone to see.
Clymer and Martin, 1978: 18

Passage B
A man named Walter Burley Griffin was asked to plan the city. It was to be called Canberra. Canberra is an Aboriginal word that means 'a meeting place'. Canberra was planned as a city where the government could make the laws of the country.
Ibid.: 26–7
Taken from Reading 360, Level 7, Book 4, *The City*, ©
Ginn and Company Limited.

2 Language as social practice

Introduction

The previous chapter introduced some ways in which language may be classified and described. It was concerned with the micro aspects of language, at and below the level of the sentence. The purpose of this chapter is to introduce some 'macro' aspects of language, to present the idea of language as social practice, and to begin to consider the significance of this for children's learning about language. We shall look at the functions of language in social interactions, considering the way language is bound up with people's social identities and their relationships to each other. The meanings created by speakers and listeners in interpersonal contexts are the focus of the approach to studying language known as 'pragmatics', which will also be considered in this chapter. We shall explore briefly the connection between the world of lived experience and the language in which it is represented. We shall also consider the notion that language is profoundly 'dialogic' – produced by people collaboratively rather than merely in individual minds. The final section of the chapter will discuss the implications for primary teachers of a description of language as social practice.

A focus on the micro aspects of language can lead to a perception that it is a single entity, something static like a scientific specimen which can be dissected and catalogued according to its separate parts (sounds, words, sentences). The danger with this conceptualization of language is that we may fall into the trap of seeing it as made up of discrete and separate pieces. This is an inaccurate perception, since language is actually acquired and used in social contexts. The consideration of language as social practice is often referred to as discourse. 'Discourse analysis' has been used to encompass a number of approaches drawing on disciplines which are concerned with the study of society and which situate language in social contexts. A view of language as discourse, as social practice, is an integral part of understanding how children learn, and learn about, language itself.

The idea of language as 'built up' from separate and discrete pieces suggests the metaphor of a jigsaw, and just such an illustration was in fact used on the cover of a 'book about words' included in a 'focus pack' on language produced by a popular teachers' journal (*Junior Education*, July 1993). Each piece was inscribed with a single word, and the pieces linked together to make up simple sentences. However, the jigsaw metaphor may help also to illustrate some of the *limitations* of teaching about language by chopping it up into little pieces. In his novel *Life, A User's Manual*, Georges Perec ruminates on the qualities of a wooden jigsaw, which:

> ... is not a sum of elements to be distinguished from each other and analysed discretely, but a pattern, that is to say a form, a structure: the element's existence does not precede the existence of the whole, it comes neither before nor after it, for the parts do not determine the pattern, but the pattern determines the parts: knowledge of the patterns and of its laws ... could not possibly be derived from discrete knowledge of the elements that compose it ... The only thing that counts is the ability to link this piece to other pieces ...
>
> Perec, 1988: xv

Similarly, as human beings we are linked through language to experiences whose meanings are irreducibly social.

The functions of language in social interaction

We can look at language and how people use it from many points of view. Some researchers, particularly those with an interest in the psychology of language development, focus on the individual pieces of the jigsaw, as it were, documenting linear sequences such as the order in which particular kinds of words are used by the individual child, or the progress from one-word to two-word expressions. Sociolinguists who are interested in the development of children's *competence* with language ask different kinds of questions. They have investigated the different functions which language performs for the young child and how, linguistically, children manage different social situations and needs. Pre-eminent among these researchers is M.A.K. Halliday, who documents the uses to which language is put, suggesting seven broad categories of function which are learned experientially at the same time as the child is learning to make use of the sounds, vocabulary and structures which make the communication of meanings possible. A functional perspective on language has implications for children learning and teachers teaching about language, and these will be explored below. First, however, a summary is presented of the functions of language as outlined in, among other places, Halliday (1982).

Very young children learn as a result of their experience that language can be deployed for the purpose of getting things done, its *instrumental* function, which includes the satisfaction of material needs, eliciting a response from those around them to the announcement 'I want . . .' Children also construct a *regulatory* model of the function of language, as their awareness develops of the fact that language can be used to influence the behaviour of others, especially through their experience of adults using language to constrain what they, as children, are permitted to do. Children discover the vital importance of language in the maintenance and development of personal relationships, its *interactional* function, and, equally, they become aware of the way in which their individuality is identified and realized through language, its *personal* function. Children's use of language to find out more about the world and their experience is labelled by Halliday as its *heuristic* function. It is particularly in this region, he suggests, that young children learn some metalinguistic terminology (i.e. language for talking about language), as their parents or other adults pass explicit comment on the fact that they ask so many 'questions', that they demand 'answers', and so on. Further metalanguage is generated in that function of language which allows children to construct alternative versions of the world, as, through the creation of 'stories' and in games of 'pretend', they derive an *imaginative* model of language. This function also includes the experience of playing with sounds, words and rhymes which may not carry any reference to meaning. And children also become aware of a *representational* model of language, the function performed by language when people communicate about something, express propositions, enact instances of 'I've got something to tell you.'

Young children, then, are learning what language is for at the same time as their knowledge of words and structures is increasing. However, the significance of a functional perspective on language extends beyond the stage of initial acquisition, and can provide material for language as curriculum content, a point which will be taken up later in this chapter and again in Chapter 7. The discussion of language as social practice extends beyond the child's early perceptions of the various functions of language, and we go on now to consider various ways in which language is bound up with social experience throughout human life.

Language and social identity

As human beings, we define ourselves in relation to other social beings, and language is intimately associated with our social identity. Halliday has captioned the personal function of language in the young child's experience as the 'here I come' function (ibid.: 46), which relates to the 'interactional function . . . of getting along with others'. We all learn to negotiate different social situations and to modify our behaviour in relation to the implicit ground rules which operate in different social contexts. One element in these adjustments is the degree of formality we adopt, exemplified by the linguistic continuum which runs from *How do you do?* to *Hi!* Some adults feel that they have been addressed inappropriately if their first name is used by a new acquaintance, rather than a title and surname. This linguistic act is perceived as a social slight, with potentially damaging consequences for the relationship. Many people make quite profound changes to the way they speak when moving from one social setting to another, in response to reactions of others to their regional accents, for example, and there are commodities on the market which promise to make you a more likeable person by equipping you with more confidence in your spoken language. Language is never neutral. People may feel that their own usages are 'natural', only to discover that to someone else a particular expression of theirs sounds quaint, holds sexist connotations, or reveals something which is considered significant about their class background.

Language can signify membership – or not – of a region, nation or religion. Most people, asked about this in their own experience, have some memory of becoming aware that their own language, particularly their way of speaking, identified them as belonging or not belonging to a social group at some level. For my part, I learned as a child to shorten the vowels in words which identified me as an outsider to the North Midlands town in which I went to school. Speaking as my parents spoke had earned me the label 'posh' and a strong desire to be included was sufficient impetus for me consciously to alter my pronunciation.

Beyond the region, national identity and the struggle of groups of people for recognition as a nation are almost always symbolized in linguistic struggles. Examples include Welsh, Catalan, Basque and the languages of the former Yugoslavia. The following extract from a recent book about sociolinguistics which is obviously dated now may be read as a prophetic illustration of this point:

> Yugoslavia is a country with three official languages: Serbo-Croatian, Slovenian, and Macedonian. However, many Croats argue that Serbian and Croatian are really separate languages and seek equal status for their language . . .
>
> They . . . equate having a different language as establishing some kind of claim for separate nationhood . . .
>
> Wardhaugh, 1992: 353, 27

Followers of Islam or Judaism, whatever their first language, learn not only the content of the respective creeds, but also the language associated with the religion. Revisions to the language in which Christian services were conducted, in the case of both Latin and archaic English, met with deeply felt opposition. The replacement of these languages with contemporary standard English could hardly have been a barrier to communication, so the reason for the opposition would seem to be an emotive connection between the language used and the community created in the membership of the religion.

The significance which language varieties have for individuals and groups, and the way in which language choices are partly constitutive of people's social identity, are matters which are often overlooked by those who seek to legislate over language. Chapter 4 will explore in more detail the controversy which has surrounded the issue of the national language and the school curriculum, but we should note here that it is a crass over-simplification of cause and effect to suppose that because people are told by authority that something is good for them they will immediately change their behaviour in the direction of the advocated policy. The fact that language is constitutive of our experience and our identity as social beings in so many complex ways makes it unlikely that simply being instructed about the 'rule' for agreement between subject and verb in standard English will be enough to make children modify their linguistic behaviour. There is often a 'covert prestige' which attaches to the use of non-standard varieties, and the cost of being criticized by teachers may be outweighed by the benefits of remaining identifiably a member of the peer group. Cheshire and Edwards (1993), who conducted a survey of school children's attitudes to these issues, concluded that 'it is extremely doubtful whether the attempts of present-day teachers to change dialect speech or writing will be any more effective than those of the past' (p. 41). Some suggestions about the ways in which these issues, rather than being ignored, might be raised as part of the language curriculum are presented in Chapter 7.

Language and social relationships

A conceptualization of language in terms of its functions requires us to look beyond the role of language in social identities and consider other ways in which language functions in social relations. If we observe young children becoming increasingly fluent speakers of their native language, and gradually learning to read and write, it is easy to imagine child and language as two separate entities, the language lying there waiting to be acquired, the child gradually 'picking up' more and more of it and deploying it in the service of its various functions. But the whole process is more organic than this, more interactional, more inherently social. Social relations are not reducible to the sum of their individual parts, as I shall try to indicate by the examples which follow.

The presence of a new member of the linguistic community, as when a new child is born into it, alters and contributes to the existing social relations in the family so that a child who is learning language is simultaneously making contributions to the linguistic interactions which are taking place. A new baby is given a name, a linguistic marker of identity, placing the child in particular relationships with those around it. Naming systems are intricately linked to social relationships, denoting family connections and sometimes memberships of other social groupings, such as a religion. The birth of a first baby changes the status of the woman who gives birth, as she becomes linguistically marked as a 'mother', while a subsequent baby makes a 'brother' or 'sister' of its siblings. The baby becomes a person who is talked about and also talked to, and the discourse of the family is altered in quite profound ways as the relationship with the growing infant becomes increasingly dialogic. The child's social horizons soon begin to extend beyond the home, and new discourses become part of the family's repertoire as the child incorporates the kinds of language used in her nursery, playground, or favourite television programme into her conversation. This whole process is an aspect of social relations and not simply an unfolding of the linguistic potential of an isolated individual.

It is not only, moreover, that language *reflects* the social relations in which children come to be participants from their earliest days. Language is itself a key medium through which social relations themselves are *enacted*. Chapter 5 takes up in more detail the significance of this for schools, but the classroom may provide us here with one brief illustration of this proposition. Suppose a pupil, Rajbinder, is known to friends and family as Raju, an affectionate contraction of his name which his teacher has come to use since he joined her class. On a particular occasion, the teacher suspects the pupil of involvement in some misdemeanour and calls him over to confront him about it, saying, 'Rajbinder, will you come here a minute, please.' The use of the more formal, official version of the name (together with a particular intonation in the utterance) not only *reflects* the kind of interaction which the teacher has chosen, it is part of what *constitutes* the social relationship between teacher and child at this moment, simultaneously showing him that there is greater distance than usual between the participants and actually creating that metaphorical distance by means of this discursive move.

Pragmatics

The above example takes us into the domain of pragmatics, the awareness people have of the meaning and significance of linguistic exchanges as they occur in actual social contexts, the intentions and presuppositions of speakers and the effects produced on listeners. Thus, in this example, *Rajbinder* 'means' (or denotes) this individual pupil, but the use of his full name 'signifies' the relation which the teacher wishes to establish between herself and him. Those who study pragmatics give us further evidence that language cannot be said to 'mean' things in a transparent and unproblematic way, but that *people* mean things by their choices of language, and those meanings are, particularly in spoken language, closely related to the social contexts in which they occur.

Learning to use language successfully includes learning, albeit not explicitly or consciously, to interpret the pragmatics of conversations, and children have to do this over a gradually increasing range of contexts, including the institutional setting of the school, which is explored in Chapter 5. There are many ways in which participants in conversations assume shared knowledge with other speakers, and they tend to follow certain conventions. We may not notice that we are absorbing the expectations of these things associated with the society in which we live, but speakers of a language do typically cooperate so that meanings can be successfully exchanged. We tend to become aware of the effects of these conventions when one or more of them are flouted, such as when someone introduces a topic which seems to other participants to be irrelevant, or when someone makes explicit information which everyone else already knows, and, depending on the norms of the culture in which it occurs, conversational behaviour of this sort among adults may be regarded as noticeably odd. Consider the example of a very young child who is just learning to use the telephone. She picks up the receiver when the telephone rings and is asked by the caller, 'Is your mummy there?' Interpreting the question as she might in other contexts, the child answers 'Yes' and hangs up. The caller is made aware that the semantic and formal meaning of his question has been appropriately understood, but that the meaning he intended, in this context, has not.

Children may bring the pragmatics of verbal interaction to our notice when they are puzzled by some aspect of spoken language in context, which will often prompt questions, particularly of parents. My own son, whose observations on language I have noted during his early childhood (Sealey, 1994), demonstrated his awareness at 4 years old of the potential for different interpretations of the same utterance, in an exchange about a meal I had prepared. As I put the dinner on the table he asked, 'Is it spicy?' to which I replied, 'Not very spicy, no.' My son's response was, ' "Not very" means it is.' Another child whose explicit comments on language were observed by his mother took offence when she remarked that his older brother was very committed to playing for a football team. 'It was the way you said it,' he told his mother, ' "*He's* so committed," as though I'm not.'

The latter incident illustrates yet another sense in which language and social relationships are intertwined. In addition to the socially sensitive communication of meanings, speakers have to negotiate the rituals which establish and limit their relationship to each other, the procedures we follow to ensure that our 'face' is not threatened and that we do not threaten the 'face' of others (Goffman, 1959; Brown and Levinson, 1978). In specific interactions, people preserve the versions of the self which are presented to others by means of various cues, many of which may be analysed from the point of view of the linguistic choices made. In addition to the bald content of conversational exchanges, such as one person seeking a favour from another, for example, people include language which maintains the relationship, surrounding a request with softeners such as *I was wondering* and *please*, and signalling awareness that the other person has the option of refusing (see McCarthy and Carter, 1994: 120). Very little research has been done into children's conscious awareness of these aspects of social interaction (see Chapter 3), but such as there is suggests that they are an important part of children's knowledge about language which they continue to learn about as other aspects of their language develop.

Language and representation

Language is often perceived as a neutral carrier of ideas between one person and another, but its pragmatic dimension draws attention to some of the problems of meaning which this perception fails to address. The same combination of words does not mean the same thing in all circumstances, nor does the same combination of words mean the same thing to all speakers. Lee (1992: 81–2) gives the example of a driver consulting a mechanic about the poor performance of his car. The mechanic says, 'It's a distributor problem.' Lee then contrasts what this utterance would 'mean' to three different interpreters, one who has an extensive knowledge of car mechanics, another who has only vague knowledge of the functioning of a car engine, and a third with no knowledge at all. For the first interpreter, the words spoken trigger a range of associations, images and implications, while the second will relate them much more schematically to existing conceptions. For the third interpreter the 'meaning' of the text is minimal. Lee asserts that we have been influenced by the metaphor for language which presents it as a kind of container in a transport system, carrying ideas between language users, where 'meanings exist as object-like entities in the minds of individuals' (ibid.: 80). He gives a number of examples of metaphorical expressions in which language is portrayed in this way, such as, 'I just can't take in what he's saying,' and we could add to the same conceptual group the example of children 'picking up' language as a metaphor for acquisition. However, we should be able to recognize, in the light of the foregoing discussion, that the communication of meaning is much more complex than this.

As has been stated before, language is a symbolic system, in which the words given to phenomena are connected only arbitrarily and by convention to the phenomena themselves. The selection of linguistic categories to which experiences and events are assigned is socially and culturally determined. One of the areas of experience which is often used to exemplify this is the language associated with gender. For example, the gender categories of male/female, girl/boy, man/woman are so integrated into the language that it is very difficult to talk about human beings without categorizing them according to gender. English has no gender-neutral pronoun, and the debate continues over whether the word *man* can really be used as a gender-free generic term and simultaneously mean an adult male human being. The convention that it can mean both accounts for apparently anomalous sentences such as, 'Man, being a mammal, breastfeeds his young.' From a lexical point of view, attention has been drawn to the fact that even apparently matched pairs of words such as *master/mistress* or *bachelor/spinster* carry quite different connotations. Consider the difference in cultural meaning between 'He became her master' and 'She became his mistress.' At the level of discourse, various studies have investigated the different ways in which females and males are written about, including the tendency for newspaper reports, for example, to assume that people are male unless proven female (the 'Androcentric Rule'; Coates, 1993). Women are also habitually defined in relation to men, so that a murder victim may be reported as 'a doctor's wife' rather than as an individual in her own right (see Lee, 1992: 112).

There are discourses which operate in an analogous way to construct particular meanings around the concept of 'the child', and there are many other ways in which language helps to determine our perception of experience, as well as reflecting it. Perspectives on events become integral to descriptions of them, so that one speaker's 'freedom-fighter' is another speaker's 'terrorist'. Written texts generated from competing views of the world will 'front' or 'foreground' different aspects of an event or situation, as comparisons between different newspaper headlines illustrate. McCarthy and Carter (1994: 157) cite two headlines which refer to events at the time of the miners' strike in Britain in 1984. The first reads, 'Coal Board closes 30 pits. Miners protest,' and the second, 'Pit closure sees violent scenes.' Among various contrasting linguistic features of these two texts, the authors draw attention to the grammatical difference between the verb form *close* and the nominalized version *closure*, which shifts attention away from the agent who performed the act of closing, the Coal Board. This device is similar to the use of the passive to conceal agency, another aspect of linguistic perspective. (A comparable example of a passive construction is when a child announces, 'This got broken', omitting the agent, 'by me'.)

There are many ways in which grammar interacts with semantics to encode certain meanings rather than others. Bolinger (1980) writes about the 'hidden propositions' in linguistic choices. Hidden propositions include the use of euphemisms, which minimize negative associations, like the affectionate or heroic names and terms used for weapons and acts of war (*Fat Man, Trident, a high rate of attrition*), or the glamourizing or understating the nature of unpleasant work by changes in job titles (*dustbin men/refuse collectors*). A speaker's stance towards an issue may be signalled by the choice from among a range of words to name the same thing. In the case of a discussion about abortion, for example, speakers (or writers) may choose either *fetus* or *unborn baby*, according to their beliefs. Differences in attitudinal meaning may be signalled by expressing the same proposition in subtly different ways. For example, suppose two teachers have been assigned to stay in the hall while a visiting theatre group performs for the school. The performance finishes at three o'clock. Afterwards, one teacher says to a colleague, 'It was over by three o'clock', and the other, in a similar conversation with a different member of staff, says, 'It went on until three o'clock.' Although the same information is conveyed in each case, the construction of the utterance allows for the incorporation of different speakers' meanings. In Chapter 1 we looked at the fact that adjectives as a grammatical class are sometimes identifiable by their form. The suffix *-able* or *-ible* usually indicates that a word is an adjective. Bolinger (1980) points out that this construction may be used to imply that people or things possess certain qualities, rather than that the speaker has certain attitudes towards them. In this way, a construction such as 'I don't like X', may become 'X is undesir*able*', or, conversely, 'I admire Y' becomes 'Y is admir*able*'.

These are just some examples of the ways in which language is far from neutral in its representation of our experiences. While teachers of primary school children would be unlikely to need to teach this degree of detail, it is important that we are aware of the role of language in social relations, and that this dimension of language teaching is not omitted from the curriculum.

The dialogic qualities of language

Much of what has been said so far in this chapter emphasizes that language is not the product of single, separate individuals, but is produced collaboratively as people interact in social contexts. Hence the term 'dialogic' as applied to language, where a dialogue between people produces discourse which is not the exclusive property or product of any one person. The Russian philosopher Bakhtin extended this notion when he reflected on the ways in which voices echo throughout texts (spoken and written) as people borrow the utterances of others and make them their own. Voices speak through another voice or voice type as language is used in social interactions:

> . . . the word does not exist in a neutral and impersonal language (it is not, after all, out of a dictionary that the speaker gets his words!), but rather it exists in other people's mouths, in other people's concrete contexts, serving other people's intentions: it is from there that one must take the word, and make it one's own.
>
> Bakhtin, 1981: 293–4

These ideas recognize that there is a process of interaction between pre-existing discourses and the potential for new meanings, as people utilize language in communication. In the case of written texts, literary criticism has been influenced by these concepts and many contemporary analysts explore the ways in which texts are more or less 'open' or 'closed'. Questions asked include how much room there is to negotiate meanings in response to a text and how far the meanings are predetermined by the kinds of discourse used. Texts 'position' their readers to make meanings dialogically. Events are described from one point of view rather than another, which offers the reader certain potential meanings rather than others. A text may use personal pronouns to address readers directly, inviting cooperation in making meaning, or it may close down potential dissent. Writers can, for example, as we saw above, choose one word or grammatical construction rather than another to encapsulate an idea about which there are alternative perceptions.

The notion of the dialogic nature of language in the social construction of the self has also been explored by some writers. Davies and Harré, for example, have considered how particular discourse situations 'position' people within social practices, rather as though they take up particular roles, such as the role of 'customer', 'teacher' or 'wife'. However, they draw a distinction between the idea of individuals taking on a 'role', freely and with the option of relinquishing it in due course, and their conception of subject positioning and its relationship to discourse:

> With positioning, the focus is on the way in which the discursive practices constitute the speakers and hearers in certain ways and yet at the same time is [sic] a resource through which speakers and hearers can negotiate new positions. A subject position is a possibility in known forms of talk; position is what is created in and through talk as the speakers and hearers take themselves up as persons.
>
> Davies and Harré, 1991: 62

In Chapter 5 we shall consider how the discourses of the school position children and teachers in particular ways, and many of the ideas introduced here will be taken up again at different points in the book. At this point, however, it is appropriate to review the distinction between micro and macro approaches to describing language, and to consider the implications for teaching about language in the primary school. Figure 1.1 is reproduced below with modifications to take account of ideas introduced in this chapter (Figure 2.1).

Language as social practice: implications for teaching

As we saw in Chapter 1, topics found in linguistic description at the micro level include phonology and orthography, lexis, grammar (morphology, word classes and syntax) and semantics. One property of texts is that they are made up of these linguistic elements. Texts may also be classified into groups with properties in common, and these groups may be thought of as 'genres'. Nunan (1993: 120, emphasis added) defines a genre as:

> a particular *type* of oral or written communication such as a narrative, a casual conversation, a poem, a recipe or a description. Different genres are typified by a particular structure and by grammatical forms that reflect the communicative purpose of the genre in question.

The inclusion of discourses in Figure 2.1 is a reminder that language is a social process, linked with social relationships and structures which are not confined to language. Thus the texts we study may be representative of various genres, and may arise within different discourses. The macro dimensions shown in Figure 2.1 enable us to consider texts as examples of language as a human practice, with social, historical and geographical dimensions and variations. Each dimension shown is again given an abbreviation, so that the examples of teaching and learning about language given subsequently in the book may be related to the topics in the figure.

Any pedagogical model for teaching about language must involve choices about which dimension to emphasize or omit, or whether to attempt to synthesize micro and macro dimensions, and how to create learning contexts for the kinds of language study chosen. The approach advocated here allows for the macro and micro dimensions to be considered simultaneously, by seeing texts as a starting point for teaching. In all four modes, the receptive modes of listening and reading, and the productive modes of speaking and writing, the National Curriculum requires that children's work with language is marked by involvement with a wide range of texts. Specific texts are inevitably produced in a social context, and provide scope for consideration of the macro aspects of language. Equally, specific texts are always realizations of meaning constituted by the micro features of which they are composed.

Children's interest in language as a ubiquitous feature of their experience in the world is as likely to be in the macro dimensions of language as in its micro features. The questions which children ask about language give an indication of the aspects which they find interesting. Very little research has been carried out into this area, but some evidence is available from an informal research project which I conducted at the University of Warwick with the help

Figure 2.1 The 'micro' and 'macro' elements of language (adapted with permission from a diagram devised by George Keith)

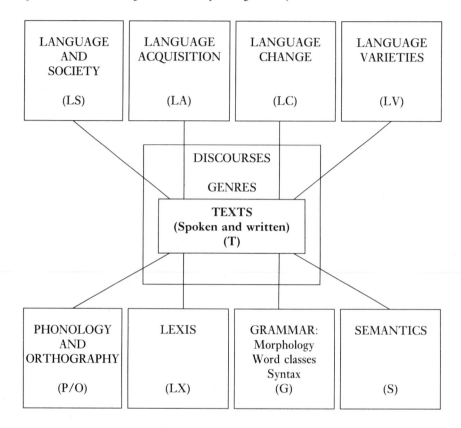

of some undergraduates who were studying to become teachers and had children themselves. They recorded questions asked and comments made by their children about language, as I have done with my own son. The questions – and the majority of the utterances recorded were questions – ranged right across the micro/macro distinction, as is illustrated by linking the examples with the different topics in Figure 2.1. One 8-year-old girl sought an explanation, just before she went to sleep one night, about the peculiarities of English spelling, asking her mother why words are not all spelt as they sound (P/O). She gave *photo* as an example and proceeded to play around with the word made by 'sounding out' the letters used to spell it, which she pronounced as *perhoetoe*. This led her to observe about the relationship between words and their meanings:

> You know funny words we say, Mummy, like flabberdyboo. Well, a word like 'spoon' could be a funny word, but it's not. That's because we know what a spoon is . . . A French person might think all our words are funny, and we would think theirs are funny, because we speak a different language.

This second line of thought, about different perceptions of words, demonstrates an awareness of language varieties (LV) but also of the attitudes held towards different languages (LS) by speakers with different language backgrounds. (It also, incidentally, hints at an embryonic perception of the arbitrariness of the connection between signifier and signified.)

Many of the children's questions concerned word meaning (S), often prompted by words heard on television and radio, which children would try to fit into a context. One 8-year-old boy was puzzled to hear that his father was going to 'transfer' him when he was asleep. His mother explained that he meant to take the child back to his own bed, but realized that her son had only understood the word up to now in the context of players being 'transferred' between football teams. The wider potential for the meanings of words is often explored when children draw attention to them in contexts like these. Sexist language (LS) was another talking point arising from different uses of the same word. One 10-year-old girl had heard the word *tart* used in a derogatory way and wanted more explanation, and a 9-year-old boy asked about *bitch*. From hearing the word used at school, his perception of its sexist meaning was more powerful than the 'literal' meaning, so that he felt uncomfortable choosing it as an example of a -*tch* word for his spelling homework (P/O).

In the context of school work, as I have said, the micro and the macro aspects of language are likely to be encountered together if the teaching about language is text based. We shall conclude this chapter by taking two examples, one of a text which children might encounter in their reading and the other a text written by children themselves.

The fiction written for children by Roald Dahl was found to be very popular in schools in a survey conducted by the researchers who evaluated the early implementation of the English National Curriculum (SCAA, 1994a). One of his novels, *The BFG* (Dahl, 1982), was referred to in Chapter 1 as a source of data about the formation of words in different classes. Like other literature which makes creative use of nonsense words, such as the writing of Lewis Carroll and Edward Lear, *The BFG* offers rich possibilities for exploring language at the level of words (LX). Children tend when they hear the story read aloud to imitate the language of the giant, and the words he uses are seductive as alternatives to words in standard English for objects and creatures. The giant eats *snozzcumbers*, drinks *frobscottle*, purveys pleasant dreams, which are *wonksquifflers* or *phizzwizards*, and censors nightmares, which are *trogglehumpers*. Morphologically, the words follow the characteristics of English words (G), managing as well, like Lewis Carroll's *slithy toves*, to suggest appropriate meanings (S).

In addition, the giant uses a peculiar version of English syntax (G), which, again, could form the focus of an interesting investigation for children. By looking closely at examples of the giant's dialogue, children could infer the 'rules' which he uses to construct his sentences. For example, the majority of the giant's sentences include the progressive present tense of the verb in the form associated in standard English with a singular, third person subject: 'We is going right past all those other giants!' (p.76) and 'Giants is only sleeping every now and then' (p. 94). The giant uses a similar construction instead of the auxiliary *do*: 'I is not wishing to know anything' (p. 65) rather than 'I don't wish to know ...' and 'Is you seeing that whopping great one ... ?' (p. 76) rather than 'Do/did you see ... ?' Children could try to construct sentences of their own in the same kind of dialect, either before or after generating its 'rules'. The terminology used in this paragraph would certainly not be needed to precede such an investigation, although you might decide to introduce it at some point.

In addition to the invented words used in this text, there are various plays on words (S), which also draw the reader into the language Dahl has deployed. The BFG explains to Sophie that the 'human beans' which the other giants eat vary in taste according to where they come from. This is an extract from their conversation:

> 'The human bean,' the Giant went on, 'is coming in dillions of different flavours. For instance, human beans from Wales is tasting very whooshey of fish. There is something very fishy about Wales.'
> 'You mean whales,' Sophie said. 'Wales is something quite different.'
> 'Wales is whales,' the Giant said. 'Don't gobblefunk around with words ...'
>
> Ibid.: 28

As children become more fluent in their native language and conscious of the cultural associations which go with words and their meanings, they some-times explore the same kind of possibilities themselves. In the parents' data described above, there are various examples of children trying to forge connec-tions rather like those made by the BFG. For example, one young child asked his mother what *summoned* meant, and she explained that it meant being told to appear in court. The child then wondered, 'Do they order you only in summer time?' My own son posed a similar question about a proposed trip to Drayton Manor Park, asking, 'Why is it called *manor*? Is it because you have to mind your manners and not touch the animals?'

However, it is disingenuous to overlook the social meanings of assigning characteristics to groups of people on the basis of national identity, the basis for the punning in *The BFG*. Although at one level this whole fantasy about the flavour of different nationalities is a harmless playing with words, readers are aware of the cultural resonances associated with a statement like, 'Greeks is all full of uckyslush. No giant is eating Greeks, ever ... Greeks from Greece is all tasting greasy' (ibid.: 26). Children can be given opportunities to discuss their views on the links between language and social judgements (LS), and a text such as this could well be a stimulus.

Similar aspects of language as a social phenomenon arose during a project in which some children in Years 5 and 6 produced a range of texts in different media. The topic for all the texts was the children's own school, but different audiences were targeted, and different aspects of the school highlighted, in the different texts produced. One group produced a radio advertisement aimed at persuading local parents to choose this school for their children. They worked collaboratively on a script, and two children translated it into Urdu, for the benefit of the many local mothers who might not understand the English version. This process generated a lot of discussion about language varieties (LV), including the choice of Urdu rather than the less prestigious dialect of Panjabi, which was also used in this community. As the girls carried out the translation, they met some problems with vocabulary, finding it difficult to be sure, for example, how to deal with the sentence from the script which ran, 'The behaviour at this school is superb.' They were uncertain about an exact translation, and considered substituting *work* for *behaviour*, but this meant that the message would be subtly altered. They found by talking to parents that good behaviour, for some, was more important in choosing a school than a high standard of work. The girls therefore consulted a more fluent Urdu speaker and eventually arrived at an acceptable translation. This challenge arose partly because the text had a specified audience, which provided a context for such a detailed exploration of lexis and semantics (LX, S).

Some other children from this group wrote to a reporter from a local radio station, inviting him to visit the school to give them advice about their tape. They also asked whether he would record their advertisement for transmission over the air. He responded positively and spent a session with the children, recording the full dual-language presentation. However, the next day, when the school was featured in a magazine programme on the local radio station, the children's advertisement was broadcast in English only, with virtually all the Urdu edited out. The children kept diaries throughout the project, and one of them who wrote about the incident expressed her reactions as follows:

> On 28th June we were on the radio. We listened to a tape of the broadcast at assembly. Mr K changed a few things. Our group took a long time to write it in Urdu and Mr K never recorded that on tape. I felt sad we took all the time for the Urdu and he never recorded it.

The issue was taken up in a subsequent class discussion (which was tape-recorded), when one of the children, herself a monolingual English speaker, strove to offer an explanation for the omission of the community language element:

> Miss, it might be because they were um, Miss I've forgot the word, but they didn't like, um, other people except whites. If they thought that other people – that, um, 'we're white and we can understand them, um, and we can't understand Urdu or Panjabi, and why should we put it on our radio because it's not, probably, well, what would we care anyway, we only wanted English?'

One of the other children, also a monolingual English speaker, was not sure whether the omission was unfair:

> . . . could be fair, because they might think that there's more English people in England than Pakistanis, and they might think that, um, Pakistanis might not listen to the radio much.

These events arose from the detailed composition, redrafting and translation of a text, with the additional benefit of an authentic audience via the radio broadcast. They demonstrate that the children, aged between 9 and 11, were quite capable of noticing and evaluating the macro issues of linguistic diversity in their local community (LV), and the social attitudes towards different languages (LS). The teaching and learning experiences provided a space for the refining and development of that knowledge.

Conclusion

This chapter has suggested some of the ways in which language may be seen as social practice, reviewing the role of discourse in our social identities and our relationships with each other. It has suggested that there is a complex relationship between language choices and representations of our experience, and that children are constantly dealing with a range of aspects of discourse as they learn more about the social world and become more fluent talkers, readers and writers. The chapter has sought to undermine the idea that language is reducible to the competence of individuals, since it has such a vital role in our dialogic understanding of experience. In reviewing the macro dimensions of knowledge about language, the chapter has suggested that teachers can incorporate the microlinguistic aspects of texts into a more contextualized approach to teaching about language. The theme of the relationship between micro and macro aspects of teaching and learning about language will be developed further in Chapters 6 and 7. The next chapter will consider in greater detail the issue of how children's awareness of language, at all levels, grows and develops. It will also apply some of the approaches outlined here to the discourse of child development.

3   Progression in learning about language: discourses of development

Introduction

The enterprise of being a primary school teacher involves responsibility for children 'making progress' in their learning as they spend time in each class, year by year. This chapter considers the nature of progress in learning about language, and what teachers might expect to see by way of development in children's metalinguistic abilities. You may remember that the term 'meta-linguistic' was introduced in Chapter 1, where it was used to denote language about language. Different researchers conceptualize *metalinguistic awareness* in slightly different ways, but they have a common interest in how children show that they know something about the characteristics of language and the way it functions – and how they know that they know it.

Like most of the issues addressed in this book, the topic of this chapter is not uncontroversial. There are different perceptions about what metalinguistic awareness is, but, more fundamentally, there are different perceptions about the whole notion of 'development', how children learn and how and why that learning should be measured. This chapter, therefore, will consider some contrasting views of learning, locating them in the context of the obligations on teachers to implement the National Curriculum. It will suggest that what we do know about how children's knowledge about language develops is limited, partly because of the perspectives from which it has been considered. We shall look briefly at what we can infer about progression from traditional textbooks, and the chapter will present some findings from psychological research into metalinguistic development, contextualizing these within the views of discourse outlined in the previous chapter. The chapter will conclude with some suggestions for primary teachers to use when considering children's progress in learning about language.

Views of learning

While the statement made at the beginning of this chapter, about teachers' responsibility for children's educational progress, may seem to be common sense, there are of course different perceptions about what constitutes learning and how development occurs. The academic discipline which has contributed most to knowledge about learning is psychology, which has investigated 'cognitive development' extensively and contributed much to education through the practical application of its findings. Primary school teachers will, for example, be familiar with the contribution made by the psychologist Piaget to our understanding of how children learn, but it is important to recognize that the description of development which derives from this tradition is one in which children are viewed more as isolated individuals than as social beings. As Bruner (1985: 26) notes, 'in the Piagetian model . . . a lone child struggles single handed to strike some equilibrium between assimilating the world to himself or himself to the world.' This tendency in psychological research to isolate individuals is compounded by a methodology which relies on experiment and measurement rather than on the observation of social interaction. We shall see below how this perspective constrains inquiry into what children know about language itself.

Just as developments in linguistic research have demonstrated the significance in descriptions of language of its profoundly social character (see Chapter 2), so in educational research there is an increasing recognition of the limitations of descriptions of intellectual development which fail to take account of social interaction. However, there is nevertheless a continuing struggle between an 'individuated' view of the child at school and a more socially contextualized view of what education is. This is partly due to the recent history of educational policy. In particular, the apparatus of assessment which is integral to the 1988 Education Reform Act requires that pupils are identified and 'marked' *as individuals*. Carter and Burgess (1993: 234), writing about Foucault's insights into the role of the school in the maintenance of social order, claim that, 'the educational order became a means of distributing individuals around certain notions of worth, rank, character and application as measured by tests and examinations, positioning individual pupils in an official hierarchy'.

The construction of all the syllabuses which constitute the National Curriculum was a political enterprise, with struggles between different perceptions of teaching and learning and between different versions of what schooling is for. It is significant that the first policy document to be published as the underpinning for the work of each subject group was that on assessment and testing (DES, 1987), which closely defined levels, sequences and stages. The government which introduced the National Curriculum as part of the Education Reform Act in 1988 was partly driven by a commitment to increasing the accountability of local education authorities, schools and teachers, so as to demonstrate that as children progressed through the school system, their parents were getting value for money. A leaflet produced for parents around the time of the first national testing programme associated with the National Curriculum (DES, 1991) makes quite explicit the concept of progress envisaged by these political priorities: 'For each subject the targets are divided into 10 levels. Each level is the same for all pupils across the country. The levels get steadily harder. So children will still be stretched as they get older and learn more.' This concept of education is summarized quite baldly later in the text: 'School, from age 5 to 16, is a journey through the target levels.' The precise requirements for learning about language, as part of the English National Curriculum, have changed in each successive version, as we shall see below, but it is important to remember that the context of 'development' described here is as applicable to this topic (now identified as 'standard English and language study') as to all the others within the framework of the 1988 Act.

There are two senses in which discourse, as defined in the previous chapter, are relevant to this consideration of learning and cognitive development. Firstly, there is the discourse which names learning in the particular ways which are currently dominant, generating a metaphor such as 'a journey through the target levels', for example, rather than one which is suggestive of collaboration or creative initiative. The second aspect of discourse to which we need to pay attention is the discourse of the classroom, where, presumably, learning takes place. This point is developed further in Chapter 5, but we need to be aware of perspectives on learning which emphasize the part played by language and discourse in the construction of shared meanings, of 'common knowledge' (Edwards and Mercer, 1987). If the view of language as a social practice, outlined in the previous chapter, is valid, then it has implications for the practice of teaching and learning, and these implications are receiving increasing recognition. Bruner (1986: 127), for example, has emphasized the critical importance of not isolating the individual learner from the cultural context:

> most learning in most settings is a communal activity, a sharing of the culture. It is not just that the child must make knowledge his own, but that he must make it his own in a community of those who share his sense of belonging to a culture. It is this that leads me to emphasize not only discovery and invention but the importance of negotiating and sharing.

In relation to what and how children learn about language, the discursive medium is particularly important. Awareness of the dialogic character of language itself, such as that derived from the work of Bakhtin, discussed in the previous chapter, may be applied to children's own learning through language. Such a process makes it very difficult to perceive the single child progressing through a narrow range of specific linguistic objectives, as is illustrated by the work of Maybin, for example. She recorded the informal talk of groups of primary school children and analysed it in relation to their construction of meanings and understandings. Among her conclusions were the following:

> Most of the talk is highly collaborative. Children complete each other's utterances, repeat something another child had just said, echo the voice of a teacher or

of a text they have been reading, and frequently use reported speech in relating incidents or anecdotes. Meanings do not seem to be generated within one mind and then communicated to another through talk; rather, they are collaboratively and interactionally constructed between people.

Maybin, 1994: 147

As we have seen, the potential for teachers to capitalize on the implications of this kind of research is somewhat limited by the statutory duty on them to make sure that individual children make their assessed individual progress through the statutorily defined 'levels'. There is some flexibility in teaching styles and in methods they may use to facilitate learning about language in interactive ways, but it is nevertheless incumbent on them to know how teaching and learning about language are defined by the 1995 version of the English National Curriculum.

Progression in learning about language in the English National Curriculum

The original English Working Group, under Professor Brian Cox, had to juggle whatever they decided would form the content of their proposals in the light of a number of interests and pressures within and outside the teaching profession. For the politicians, knowing about language meant knowing the rules of grammar (see Cox, 1991), while educational practitioners had good reason to fear that a specific strand on knowledge about language would amount to a narrow, restrictive and possibly unworkable element of the English curriculum. The Working Group dealt with the pressure of this pincer movement by deciding not to include knowledge about language as a separate profile component, to be separately assessed. The main justification given for this was an indication of its integration 'in the speaking, listening, reading and writing activities of any English lesson' (DES, 1989: 6.2). The other reasons given for not separating it into a separate component – at least in the first instance – were the dangers of curriculum overload (ironically, in the light of the Dearing review (Dearing, 1994)), and the perceived limitations of teachers' own knowledge about language. The report acknowledged, however, the disadvantage to this structure: 'that knowledge about language can appear fragmented and that teachers and pupils might not see the possibilities for coherent and cumulative work' (ibid.: 6.4). So the original National Curriculum Order, which was based on this report, did not explicitly set out a sequence for knowledge about language as such, but instead implied that this would be found throughout the programmes of study and attainment targets. The chapter of the report which outlines the rationale for this aspect of the curriculum explains, 'A systematic approach to language study can be developed by considering any aspect of language in terms of its forms and meanings, its social uses and effects, and how it varies' (ibid.: 6.17).

One outcome of the decision to integrate knowledge *about* language with those aspects of English which are concerned with *using* language is that the two kinds of 'knowledge' have remained rather confused. The series of documents which have at various points constituted the statutory and proposed National Curriculum for English have failed to make clear exactly what constitutes children's progress in knowledge about language. There is knowledge of terminology, such as 'sentence', and knowledge of form, such as the graphical conventions of written sentences. However, what remains unspecified is whether there is conceptual knowledge which must be consciously available to children in order for them to use these terms or produce writing with these conventions, and, if so, what that knowledge is.

The sequence of progression and development of knowledge about language in the English National Curriculum is not neatly and explicitly revealed by the original statutory Order, particularly as it relates to children working at levels earlier than Level 5. For children at Key Stage 3, the second report of the English Working Group (DES, 1989) indicates a view of progression through a sequence for the child as a student of language in the final paragraph of Chapter 6:

> Pupils' developing understanding is marked in several ways:
>
> It is usually easier to give examples from local varieties of English (in the family or local community), than to discuss a wider range of varieties, which are more distant, geographically, socially or historically.
>
> It is usually easier to talk about language, than to write about it.
>
> It is usually easier to give examples of individual words (which distinguish dialects, styles, etc), than to give examples of pronunciation, grammar and textual organization.
>
> It is easier to give relevant, but isolated, examples than to give more systematic and sustained descriptions and analyses; and description is easier than discussing the principles underlying the examples.
>
> The ordering of the statements of attainment in knowledge about language takes account of this pattern of development.
>
> Ibid.: 6.21

An assumption in this list of ways in which pupils' developing understanding is marked is that a central concept which pupils will develop is that language varies – over time, in different regions and for different purposes – and that what will develop as children become more sophisticated in their understanding about language are the resources available to them to describe and analyse this variation. The revision of the Order for the English National Curriculum in 1995 brought the much more specific, sentence-level, grammatical knowledge about language to the fore and revised the general tenor of the Cox Report and the original Order, so that there was considerably less emphasis on learning about linguistic variation and about discourse processes and whole texts.

From its earliest stages, the English National Curriculum has been subject to a series of proposed revisions, consultation procedures, revised revisions, and so on. The aspect of the curriculum concerned with children's knowledge about language has had a high priority in these revisions, and yet as changes have been mooted, little evidence has been publicly put forward to provide an educational rationale for the alterations. The 1995 version incorporates the more explicit section within each attainment target of 'Standard English and Language Study', which had been defined as 'aspects of linguistic knowledge, such as grammar, vocabulary, standard English and language in use' (SCAA, 1994b: iii). Far greater space is given to standard English than in the original Order, but a sequence of progression in knowledge about language is still not explicitly presented. An early exhortation, in the programmes of study at Key Stage 1, is that:

> Pupils should be introduced with appropriate sensitivity to the importance of standard English . . . They should be introduced to some features that distinguish standard English, including subject–verb agreement and the use of the verb 'to be' in past and present tenses.
>
> DFE, 1995: 5

The conceptual knowledge specified here is at the level of the social importance of a particular version of the English language as a whole. It is not clear whether the introduction of the 'features that distinguish standard English' is to be by example, with or without the relevant terminology and within what conceptual framework of linguistic description, if any. For Key Stage 2 (ibid.: 12), the document expresses a belief that involving children in contexts which require standard English will lead to its adoption, although exactly what constitutes increasing knowledge of these features is, as ever, difficult to determine. The fact that 'standard English' is, in any case, not one homogeneous variety (an idea which will be explored further in the next chapter) is not addressed. The causal relationship between the topics twinned in this document as 'Standard English and Language Study' is also unclear. In other words, does using particular linguistic forms make it possible to be aware of their nature, or should one be taught the required construction and then put it to use? These are questions to which we shall return in later chapters.

Some particular types of knowledge about language feature in the programme of study for reading, including, at Key Stage 1, phonic knowledge, graphic knowledge, word recognition, grammatical knowledge and contextual understanding, a sequence which is familiar from Chapter 1. Somewhat surprisingly, however, these segments of *knowledge* are presented as 'Key *Skills*' (ibid.: 6–7). The section on Standard English and Language Study refers to variation in texts and the opportunities provided by reading to develop understanding of standard English. Longer stretches of language feature in the Key Stage 2 programme of study 'key skills', with the introduction of terminology with which to discuss texts marking progress in the section on Language Study and Standard English.

Some of the most explicit requirements for knowledge about language are to be found in the programme of study for writing. Here, at Key Stage 1, children are to be taught 'the connections between speech and writing', about 'the alphabetic nature of writing' and 'about the different purposes and functions of written language' (ibid.: 9). The required skills in spelling, punctuation and handwriting are enumerated. As well as the customary emphasis on standard English, pupils are to be taught:

> to apply their existing linguistic knowledge . . . to develop their understanding of the sentence and how word choice and order are crucial to clarity of meaning. Pupils should be given opportunities to discuss the organization of more complex texts, and the way sentences link together.
>
> Ibid.: 10

Similar areas of linguistic knowledge are identified for Key Stage 2, where:

> Pupils should be given opportunities to develop their understanding of the grammar of complex sentences, including clauses and phrases. They should be taught how to use paragraphs, linking sentences together coherently. They should be taught to use the standard written form of nouns, pronouns, verbs, adjectives, adverbs, prepositions, conjunctions and verb tenses.
>
> Ibid.:16

As I have said, it is not clear whether this terminology is to be taught, nor whether children need to know how to classify these elements. It is not a straightforward matter, then, to discern from National Curriculum documents exactly what learning *about* language comprises, nor is it always clear how children's progress is to be marked. However, there is a general tendency for the prescriptions of these curriculum documents to suggest development from small to larger units of meaning.

Assumptions of progress which underlie teaching materials

The emphasis on sentence grammar and on moving from smaller to larger units of meaning as a logical path of progress in children's metalinguistic development is reflected in textbooks aimed at the primary school market. For example, a popular scheme produced in 1979 for use in primary schools is the *Nelson Grammar* series of textbooks (Ballance and Ballance, 1979). Book 1 features work on the letters of the alphabet, on plural endings, on nouns, verbs and adjectives, and on simple sentences. In Book 2, conjunctions are introduced, as are pronouns, and the work on sentences revises simple sentences but also deals with 'expanding simple sentences' and with 'compound sentences'. Progress on to Book 3 is indicated by the introduction of 'auxiliary verbs' and 'the infinitive', and combinations of words at the level of 'sentences, clauses and phrases'. By the time pupils reach Book 4, concepts such as transitive and intransitive verbs appear, and there is work on the order of clauses in complex sentences. The approach used is interesting for various reasons, including the pedagogical assumptions which are implicit in the introductions to the material and the exercises which are set. However, it is of interest in this discussion of progress and development in children's explicit knowledge of language because, like later versions of the National Curriculum, with their content statutorily divided into stages and levels, it draws on the body of knowledge into which language has traditionally been classified and subdivided, and implies that progress for the learner is progress from small to larger units and from simpler to more complex combinations of words. The relationship between language and meaning is, to say the least, underemphasized, and whole texts are eschewed in favour of short passages apparently contrived to illustrate particular teaching points. Many other textbook approaches share similar features.

Research into the development of children's metalinguistic awareness

Another approach to finding out how children's knowledge about language develops is to consider the learner rather than the material to be learned. This involves studying either the same children over periods of time or children of different ages engaged in similar interactions so as to observe and analyse the changes which take place: in this case, changes in their explicit awareness of language itself. One of the difficulties in this kind of research is for the researchers to access children's consciousness of language and how it is being used, since, as we have seen, it is possible to 'know how' to do things with language without necessarily 'knowing what' we are doing. As Clark (1978: 17) points out, 'People can be aware of their language at many different levels, from the automatic, virtually unconscious monitoring of their own speech to the rapid switching of languages by professional translators to the detailed analytic work of linguists.'

A much greater amount of research has been done into children's developing competence with language than into the development of consciousness about it. One of the reasons for this is that the former is much easier to observe. For example, anyone who spends time with a young child learning to talk is likely to witness the typical sequence in which this occurs. In the earliest stages, children interact as though in dialogue with their carers, progressing through the babbling phase and use of particular sound patterns as word-like indicators of meaning, on into recognizable one-word utterances, which evolve into short phrases, until children are attempting longer constructions and moving towards use of the same grammatical structures as are used by the other people in their speech community. Such observations do not, however, answer questions about children's conscious and explicit knowledge about language. These issues require the distinction between 'knowing how' and 'knowing that'. By far the greatest amount of work in this latter area has been carried out by researchers studying children's cognitive development, and this has affected the kinds of questions asked, the assumptions underlying the research, and the methods used to find out what children know about language.

An important emphasis in many teaching programmes, such as those generated by the LINC (Language in the National Curriculum) project, to teach children about language has been on developing children's ability to *reflect* on these things, and this kind of research seeks evidence of children doing just that – reflecting on the characteristics and functions of language. Another way of thinking about this is to draw the distinction between the *medium* and the *content* of language, being aware that what people say is not exactly the same thing as how they say it. As children grow more fluent and capable as language users, how do they also show that they are aware of and are monitoring the process of producing language? Monitoring the production of language, particularly spoken language, goes on all the time, although there is debate about whether this is conscious or not. Even very young children sometimes correct themselves when they are talking if they choose the wrong word or realize that they have not made their meaning clear. However, it is possible to carry out these self-repairs, and to hear those of other people, without really noticing them at all. The research reviewed in this section is concerned with children's ability to separate linguistic form from its content at a conscious level.

Because of the emphasis on studying cognition, developmental psychologists working in the field of metalinguistic awareness have usually tried to isolate particular aspects of the phenomena they are studying, which leads both to defining very specific aspects of language as the area of investigation and also to trying to isolate the 'subject' and his or her responses and behaviour. In practice, this has led to research into children's metalinguistic awareness which places individual children in experimental situations where they are required to participate in experiments designed to demonstrate quite precisely whether they have conscious knowledge of some aspect of language. There are examples of more 'naturalistic' data, but the methods used usually involve taking children into quasi-laboratory conditions and setting up situations which, it is hoped, will show unequivocally whether the child is conscious of particular things. Sometimes, the researchers will include training sessions in a series of experiments, with the aim of ensuring that the children are clear about what is expected of them. One problem of working with young children is that they may be conscious of something and yet not be able to express that conscious awareness clearly. An analogy would be testing preliterate children's eyesight: opticians have to use pictorial symbols rather than letters so as to be sure that they are testing a child's ability to see rather than his or her ability to read. Psychologists interested in children's metalinguistic development have to find language for communicating with their subjects which conveys what they are interested in in an accessible way. Thus in asking children to identify whether given sentences are 'grammatical' or not, they may ask which ones are 'all mixed up', and children may identify sentences which 'sound wrong': the very language of the experiment thus becomes implicated in determining levels of metalinguistic awareness.

Phonological awareness

Many accounts of the range of studies into children's metalinguistic awareness start with research into phonological awareness; that is, they review the smallest units of language first. Typically, children from a range of age groups are asked to identify phonemes or syllables, sometimes being asked how many sounds there are in a series of words said aloud by the researcher, sometimes being asked to identify the individual phonemes in a given syllable. For example, Calfee *et al.* (1973) asked children from 6 to 17 years old to listen to various sequences of the phonemes /i/ and /p/. The combinations included sounds such as *pi*, *ip*, *pip*, and so on. The children had some cubes of different colours which were meant to represent the different phonemes, and they had to place them in the correct order for each combination. The experiments increased in difficulty, and the authors report on the ages at which children demonstrated greater success. By and large, the work produced in this kind of developmental psychology is not concerned with the *meaning* of language tasks like this. Researchers recognize children's own experimentation with language, as when they play with the sounds of words, particularly in rhymes and speech games, but they are reluctant to transfer conclusions from this to statements about 'true' metaphonological ability, which must, for them, be distinguished by conscious knowledge of separate sounds and combinations of sounds.

The important element of these studies for teachers working to develop children's metalinguistic ability is the link between awareness of sounds and learning to read. This is an area which is receiving increasing attention and, although we shall return to the role played by literacy in children's knowledge about language, there is not the space in this book to go into great detail. Conclusions which emerge from reviewing many studies of this area, though, are that children develop an increasing capacity to analyse language at the phonemic level from the age of 5 to 6 years onwards, and that metaphonological behaviour and the first stages of reading seem to be linked:

> learning to read and phonological awareness develop in interaction with each other. On the one hand, phonological awareness seems to facilitate learning to read; while on the other hand, progress in reading seems to facilitate the ability to divide the spoken word into segments.
>
> Gombert, 1992: 33

Metalexical and metasemantic development

There are other studies of children's metalinguistic awareness which seek to identify the sequence by which children become aware of the concept of 'the word'. You may remember that in Chapter 1 we looked at some of the ways in which implicit knowledge about words may be made explicit in the context of solving crossword clues. Researchers seeking to know what kind of concept of the metalinguistic term 'word' is held by children at a particular age define what they are looking for in quite precise terms (see Bowey and Tunmer, 1984). There has to be awareness of the word as a unit of language. It is also important that the child is aware that the sounds used in uttering the word have no intrinsic relationship with the concept conveyed by the word. In other words, the 'sign' (or word) is connected in an arbitrary way with that which it signifies. So, for example, the word *cow* does not itself have udders, make a mooing sound, or stand on four legs. And there is no reason why the animal which has those attributes should not be called *vache* (as it is in French) or *Kuh* (as it is in German). Thus metalinguistic awareness of words includes awareness of their status as arbitrary phonological labels. Children also have to understand the metalinguistic term *word*.

In Chapter 1, the distinction was drawn between lexical words and grammatical words, that is words as labels which refer to something 'in the world', and words which have a grammatical job such as indicating how the concepts conveyed by the lexical words relate to each other. Experiments suggest that it is at about 6 to 7 years of age that children begin to see lexical words as words, although they seem to have more difficulty in seeing grammatical words as words. Garton and Pratt (1989) suggest that this may be because the meaning of such words in isolation is too abstract for the child to grasp. (How would you yourself explain the meaning of the words *if*, *why* or *than*? If these were the answers to crossword clues, what would the clues be? They could not easily be synonyms!)

Piagetian experiments with young children have led researchers to believe that at first children think of the name of an object as being one of its intrinsic properties, like its colour or shape, rather than appreciating that the words used to refer to things come from the socially constructed systems of language. Children also demonstrate some confusion about the meaning of 'the word' in finding it difficult to separate properties of the words themselves from properties of the things to which they refer. Thus researchers report that when children were asked to give an example of 'a long word', they would suggest something like *train*, or *chair*, explaining that the latter was chosen 'because it has long legs to hold it up' (Berthoud-Papandropoulou, 1978: 58). Asked to give an example of a short word, suggestions included *primrose*, 'because it's small'.

Metasyntactic development

It is only when children have the ability to distinguish between language and lived experience that metalinguistic knowledge is likely to be meaningful to them, and the research in this tradition suggests that the age of about 6 to 7 is an important transitional stage. Similar findings emerge when the linguistic unit under review is at the level of syntax. Researchers have asked children of different ages to make judgements about the acceptability of various sentences, sometimes using different puppets who 'say' sentences with different structures, some of which scramble the expected word order. Younger children apparently react to the content of what is said rather than the form in which it is expressed. Children sometimes reject sentences which are grammatically correct because they are not 'true', in terms of their own experiences of the world. For example, a 4-year-old child rejected the sentence 'Yesterday Daddy painted the fence' because 'Daddies don't paint fences; they paint walls' (Tunmer and Grieve, 1984: 99–100). 'It is not until 6–7 years of age that the child becomes capable of separating the form of a sentence from its content and basing judgements on linguistic criteria alone' (Gombert, 1992: 48).

Metatextual development

Researchers have explored the development of children's awareness of the features of longer stretches of language, including complete texts. One of the ways in which texts convey coherent meaning is by the appropriate use of connectives and other markers of cohesion, and the ability to make increasing use of these features of language is required in the National Curriculum. The experimental approaches outlined above have also been used to investigate children's conscious knowledge of these aspects of texts, and the results suggest that the ability to articulate how cohesive features work in texts develops relatively late, after the stage at which children show that they can handle them in their own writing.

Implications for teaching about language

Before we leave this review of studies in metalinguistic development, it is important to note that what has been said about the social, interactive, dialogic nature of language has implications for the kind of psychological studies reviewed. The experiments which have been used are themselves discursive situations. If it is the case that children are social actors, learning from their experiences of relationships with other social beings about what it is that different discursive situations require from them, then they will be active in making meaning in the social situation of the psychological experiment too. Donaldson (1978) drew attention to this in her reformulation of Piagetian experiments so that they made 'human sense' to children, finding that the children were far less different from adults than had been supposed. It seems likely that there are limits to what we can find out about children's understanding of language as it is most frequently used – in authentic social interactions – if we study it in contrived and unusual experimental settings.

However, there are some very general conclusions about the development of metalinguistic awareness summarized here which would seem to be helpful for teachers planning teaching about language. One common finding is that the ability to reflect consciously on language itself lags slightly behind the ability to use it. A second point is that in a large number of the relevant studies, it is at about the age at which children start junior school that metalinguistic awareness is apparent, and, thirdly, the evidence reviewed suggests that the process of learning to read and write has a central role in its development. As Gombert (1992: 190) says, in his wide-ranging review of the field, 'the subject becomes aware in a "meta" (i.e. conscious) sense only of those aspects of language which *have to be* apprehended in such a way if the new linguistic tasks demanded of him or her are to be accomplished' (original emphasis).

To summarize what has been said so far: several traditions, in linguistics, in education and in psychology, may encourage us to think of children's language awareness progressing in a certain way, from smaller towards larger units, and within each child as an isolated individual. A prescribed curriculum which must by law indicate levels in a sequential way inevitably encourages us to view progress as linear rather than recursive, and textbooks also, despite their sections on 'revision', tend to reinforce a view of the individual child making his or her way along a prescribed path of development. The final section of this chapter will attempt to combine what has been said in this and the previous two chapters about microlinguistic and macrolinguistic awareness by offering some suggestions for thinking about the progression children might be expected to make in their primary school years.

Three axes of progression in learning about language

In this and the previous chapter, we have explored the limitations of a model of progression in learning about language which moves in a linear way from small to larger units of language, or an incremental model which sees increased aptitude in the naming of the elements of the language as evidence of development. An alternative perception, which will be developed here, is that there is progress to be made at both macro and micro levels simultaneously, and that the teacher who is responsible for teaching primary school children will need to be alert to the progress being made on a number of fronts at the same time. What is it that characterizes the awareness and understanding of language of a child in, say, Year 2, as compared with those of the same child about to leave the junior school at the end of Year 6? If we reject a model of discrete developmental stages, and the 'journey through the levels' which suits bureaucracy better than it does social beings, what do we have to guide us instead? Bruner (1986: 68), considering the contribution made to our understanding of children's development by post-Piagetian research, suggests that many of the skills which all human beings need in order to function as members of society, including linguistic competence, are available to even young children – provided that they perceive meaning in the interactions in which they are involved. He puts it this way: 'when a child understands the event structure in which he is operating he is not that different from an adult. He simply does not have as grand a collection of scripts and scenarios and event schemas as adults do.'

As communicators, children struggle with much the same challenges throughout their primary school careers as they will in their later education and on into their adult lives (unless, of course, they are unfortunate enough to find that their school demands a disproportionate amount of 'meaning-free' reading and writing). Many things do grow and develop, of course, but it is helpful to see these as resources available to the growing child from within the collective culture, as much as to perceive them as an unfolding of his or her individual attributes.

This section will suggest three axes along which teachers may expect to see progression, and in relation to which they can plan teaching which will help children to learn more about language. The first axis is experience, the second is precision, and the third is the degree of abstraction with which children can manipulate linguistic concepts. We shall look at each of these in turn.

Experience in learning about language

One resource available to children is their experience in the world, the growing range of people they meet, the communicative situations with which they have to deal and the vocabulary which can be used to name a wider range of phenomena. New experiences will make demands in the context of an increasing degree of independence. Thus suppose children in Year 6 take part in a school trip which involves staying away from home overnight. They may find themselves sharing accommodation in a study centre with a party from another school in another part of the country. This experience places greater communicative demands on the children than the day trip they undertook in Year 2 to a closer location with a known group of people.

The range of texts and types of text in which children are able to take a meaningful interest is greater as they progress through the school. They can be expected to look back with understanding at the format and features of picture books after they have learned to find satisfaction from more demanding literature in the upper junior years, but there are limits to what the less experienced reader can be expected to cope with when looking forwards towards the kinds of text which are intended primarily for more competent readers. Children's experience and understanding of literacy generally should be growing throughout their time in school, so that the Year 2 child who is at the stage of placing a heavy reliance on phonic strategies for spelling will have a more limited knowledge base on which to draw when set investigative tasks about language at the level of words. However, the principle that children should investigate what they already know, and also extend that knowledge by widening their experience with different examples and texts which challenge narrow stereotypes, is valid with even the youngest pupils.

Linguistic experiences will extend to include school, clubs, meetings, family occasions and an ever-increasing range of texts – songs, videos, computer games, posters, packaging, instructions for new toys and games, the letters which arrive at home and so on. All these resources add to the young child's growing 'collection of scripts, scenarios and event schemes' (Bruner, 1986: 68) and to their knowledge of discourses and texts. Greater ranges of meaning and connotations come to cluster round individual words, catch phrases, kinds of social interaction, and so on. So long as the language curriculum continues to be meaningful, children will develop, both within school and beyond, a more certain sense of what to expect and of the options open to them, including choices about what might be appropriate and effective linguistically.

Precision

Alongside developing experience goes the teacher's expectation that there will be more precision, that children's metalinguistic progression is marked by a move from broader brushstrokes towards finer attention to detail. Let us take as an illustration one topic which could well feature in the knowledge about language curriculum. In Chapter 6 it will be suggested that an important skill which helps children to learn about language is gained through experience in the classification of language. One example of doing this is in relation to whole texts, and it has been used with learners across a wide age range. Teachers and coordinators who worked with the LINC (Language in the National Curriculum) project used the experience of classifying texts with teachers on in-service courses, with secondary school students and with pupils in both junior and infant schools. In each case, the aim was to compare and contrast a group of whole (written) texts in order to draw attention to the significance of one or more of the categories which can be applied to all texts: format, function, audience, content and context. The kinds of text used in this activity vary, but they are always selected so that they will be reasonably familiar and meaningful to the group involved. Younger children might choose the texts themselves, found at home or on their journey to school (Rogers, 1991). Haynes (1992) suggests that the teacher should collect examples, photographing those which cannot be moved, and suggests: 'the lollipop lady's "STOP", "Macdonalds", street names, notices such as "Toilets", cornflakes and other packets, cartons and wrappers' (p. 100). Older children and adults have been asked to look through their pockets or bags and supply the real texts themselves – bus tickets, lesson timetables, shopping lists, diaries, and so on. A teacher of 4–6 year-olds (Rogers, 1991: 22) wanted to begin to establish the basic idea that written language in the environment has a purpose, and was gratified when one of the children noticed a range of texts, and:

> told us all about the road sign, writing on drain covers, and the bus stop. Another boy, Michael, came in one morning pleased to tell us that he had noticed six lots of language at the front of our school. This prompted me to talk about why this language was there, who it was for, and together we discovered about audience, function and format.

This activity encourages the children to think about these categories, and will be built on with greater sophistication. For instance, some children in Years 2 and 3 described by Clarke (1991) were required to write answers to questions about photographed texts and their authors such as: 'Why did they put the writing there?' and 'Why did they write it in the way they did?' We would expect children in the age group of 10 and 11 to be working at a more sophisticated level still, with children comparing, for example, the different intentions behind different types of text about the same subject, as they did in the media project described at the end of the previous chapter, or, in another example, in the context of a topic about environmental protection (Rawson, 1990), where the teacher included poetry, articles from newspapers and information from environmental groups in the texts under scrutiny. In each case, children's ability to answer the question 'How do you know?' (about the intended audience, or the genre, for example) should be given opportunities to develop.

This kind of progression is not, of course, linked inextricably to age, but rather to opportunities to learn through experience. Children who attend a school where whole-text approaches to teaching and learning about language are well established from the early years onwards will have incorporated such ideas as the variation of texts according to format, purpose, audience and context into their knowledge base and can be expected to work with greater sophistication on a wider range of texts as they go through the school. Those to whom these ideas and approaches are less familiar may come in at a different point and need to cover the ground which for others may be taken for granted.

Something else which is established as children undertake this kind of activity at an appropriate level is the *principle* of classification as being one of the things which can be done with language (see Chapter 6). This should transfer to examples other than collections of whole texts. For example, teachers might extend the experience to ask: How could we classify the new words we have learned in connection with this term's topic? Alphabetically? Semantically? Grammatically? Which would be most useful to us in the future? To another group? What will we call the categories? Children with a firm grounding in the principle of classifying instances of real language for authentic purposes would be expected to answer such questions more confidently than those to whom this process is new.

Abstraction

A third axis of progression is the level of abstraction at which ideas about language are handled. The principle of dealing with whole texts in meaningful contexts for authentic purposes applies throughout the primary school years, and this is partly because children are more likely to be successful in their work with language if it is solidly grounded in meaningful experience. This is the reason for offering as many opportunities as possible for literally handling language, providing texts which look as much like their counterparts in the real world as possible. (As an adult, you can be asked to visualize the actual text from the words I used above to describe a photograph of crossing patrol's 'STOP'; children will benefit from not having to engage in the same abstraction.) Many of the teaching examples given later in this book require operations to be carried out on texts – physically sorting them into groups and labelling each one, making actual books or taped broadcasts rather than merely producing the content of a story or report in an exercise book, cutting up and reordering texts so that the effects can be seen in fact rather than imagined in the mind. The level of sophisticated appreciation of particular knowledge about language is likely to be greater if other variables and abstractions are kept 'out of the way' of the linguistic considerations. More experienced learners continue to be entitled to work with authentic texts, and to handle them, to witness the effect of changes and reordering, but the degree of authenticity in what they produce should increase: an upper junior child's attempt to recreate the style of a newspaper headline can be expected to show more confident handling of a consistent range of the appropriate linguistic features than that of a 6-year-old, for example. Thus Slater (1992) reports on children in Year 2 successfully converting the tale of *The Three Little Pigs* into a newspaper story, and remarks on their appropriate omission of the definite article in headlines such as, 'Is Pig Safe?' and, 'Third Little Pig tells his story'. Some 11-year-olds who produced their own front page on the theme of pollution chose as one headline, 'Motorway pile-up causes oil spill: 100's of villagers at risk'. This formulation, which reads quite authentically, omits not only articles, but also a verb in the second section, whose causal connection to the first part of the headline is concisely implied by means of the colon.

Increasing precision and sophistication as markers of progression apply to awareness and manipulation of all dimensions: the forms, functions, contents and audiences of texts, written and spoken, and relationships between them, which are all developing with children's greater experience. For example, it is not that a younger child does not know that language can be used for deceptive purposes, that not all linguistic messages (including those they produce themselves) are 'true', or even unambiguous, that advertisers, for instance, may emphasize certain things about their products and omit to mention others. What children should be learning about these aspects of language, however, as they progress through primary school, is a greater degree of subtlety in responding to or creating texts which convey more than one meaning.

Conclusion

This chapter has considered how dominant 'discourses of development' encourage a perception of progress in learning which emphasizes the individual, on the one hand, and the assessable curriculum, on the other. The chapter has looked at the sequences of progress in primary children's learning about language which is implied by the English National Curriculum and by traditional textbooks, and at the findings of psychological studies of children's metalinguistic development, and I have indicated some of the limitations of these sources. Finally, I have suggested that it is possible to view progression in children's learning about language both microlinguistically and macrolinguistically, and that three dimensions would be significant: linguistic experience, precision in linguistic description and analysis, and the level of abstraction at which linguistic concepts are understood. The next chapter explores further the controversies surrounding a prescribed curriculum for learning about language, putting them into a historical perspective.

4 Knowledge about language: controversy in the curriculum

Introduction

A class of 10-year-old children studied a range of dictionaries as part of a project in which they compiled their own. They explored a little of the history of dictionaries, and discussed an extract from Dr Samuel Johnson's explanation of some of the principles he observed in compiling his own work. One of the children asked whether Johnson had had to obtain government permission to publish his dictionary. Further discussion revealed that the children were aware in various ways of the fact that the printed word could provoke controversy, and had a sense that the government might perceive itself as the arbiter of the meanings of words. A few months after this classroom lesson took place, education ministers announced a worldwide ban on publication of the materials they had commissioned to teach teachers about language (the materials from the Language in the National Curriculum project).

This chapter explores why teaching about language is controversial – why decisions about what to teach and how to teach it are inevitably taken in the context of fiercely contested opinions and attitudes. I shall argue that teachers cannot escape these controversies, because their work is carried out in a social and historical context in which the nature and the purpose of the school curriculum are both contested areas. At the same time, language is a central component in, and means of expression of, social relationships, and as such it too is a site of conflict and disagreement. Small wonder, then, that knowledge about language as a curriculum area has been the subject of fierce argument and continues to provoke strongly worded expressions of opinion. This chapter takes each topic, firstly language and then schooling, and explores some of the reasons for their controversial character. It reviews the history of the two topics combined as knowledge about language in the school curriculum, and concludes by considering the issue of standard English in relation to the 1995 English National Curriculum.

One theme recurs throughout this discussion of language and of education. In both spheres, there is a tradition of constructing and then maintaining a notion of two kinds of people: insiders and outsiders, 'us' and 'them'. And in both spheres too is a tradition of depicting the order and standards made and held by the in-group as constantly under threat from the forces of disorder outside. For teachers to appreciate the meaning and significance of their teaching about language, some awareness of the effects of these beliefs is indispensable.

Attitudes to language

> Because language is a fundamental part of being human, it is an important aspect of a person's sense of self; because it is a fundamental feature of any community, it is an important aspect of a person's sense of social identity.
>
> DES, 1989: para. 6.18

That language is inextricably linked to people's 'sense of self' can be illustrated in many ways, and is a theme which was explored in Chapter 2. As 'a fundamental feature of any community', language is expected to signify membership of a social group, and, by extension, to identify those who do *not* 'belong'. (This idea, too, was developed in Chapter 2.) Political beliefs often focus on the state of the language, as we shall see when we look at public commentary on the teaching of English, below. Here are two commentators on the state of contemporary English. The first is Keith Waterhouse writing in the *Daily Mail* on the day one of the revisions of the English National Curriculum was announced; the second is the Prince of Wales addressing a church congregation about revisions to the language of the Bible and the Book of Common Prayer:

> Even quite educated people converse in grunts and monosyllables. Sentences are unfinished, words clipped of their endings, consonants slurred or ellipsised altogether. As for street corner language, it is largely incomprehensible except to the barbarians regurgitating their oath-bespattered gobbets of verbal gristle.
>
> Waterhouse, *Daily Mail*, 10 September 1992

> Looking at the way English is used in our popular newspapers, our radio and television programmes, even in our schools and theatres, they [a great many people] wonder what it is about our country and our society that our language has become so impoverished, so sloppy and so limited – that we have arrived at such a dismal wasteland of banality, cliche and casual obscenity.
>
> The Prince of Wales, as reported in the *Daily Telegraph*, 19 December 1989, quoted in Crowley, 1991: 9

Both extracts express sentiments which have a long history. To deplore the perceived decline in the way language is used is nothing new. In 1672, for example, Dryden proclaimed the superiority of contemporary English over that available to Shakespeare and Jonson, but conceded that, 'many are of a contrary opinion, that the English tongue was then in the height of its perfection; that, from *Jonsons* [sic] time to ours, it has been in a continual declination' (quoted in Bolton, 1966: 57).

Jonathan Swift, in 1712, complained that:

our language is extremely imperfect; that its daily improvements are by no means in proportion to its daily corruptions; that the pretenders to polish and refine it have chiefly multiplied abuses and absurdities; and that in many instances it offends against every part of grammar.

Quoted in Crystal, 1987: 4

This persistent belief in language decline involves some interesting assumptions, which are not always made explicit. One assumption is that change is synonymous with decline. This belief is so taken for granted that it warrants attention, because it highlights the difference between prescriptive and descriptive stances in discourse about language. From studying language in use, and in seeking to describe it, linguists are obliged to accept that language is changing all the time, at all levels, including both the microlinguistic elements of phonemes, lexis, morphemes, syntax and semantics, and the macrolinguistic dimensions of discourse.

Examples of changes at each of these levels would include: the loss of distinction between the pronunciation of *horse* and *hoarse*, or the introduction of a distinction between the pronunciation of *house* as a noun and *to house* (phonemic change); new words (neologisms) which come into the language to meet a need to name new phenomena, such as *laser, sari, ragga* music, *Thatcherite* economics, and the loss of words which name archaic objects or whose meanings are expressed in other ways (lexical change); the replacement of the *-eth* form of the third person singular verb with *-s*, so that *she cometh* has changed to *she comes* (morphological change); new structures such as the use of *they* as a singular pronoun, to avoid the use of *he* when the gender of the person is not known; the use of *to be* followed by a verb ending in *-ing* to form the progressive: *What are you reading?*, rather than *What do you read?* (see Aitchison, 1991) (syntactic change); changes in the meanings of words over time – the word *nice*, for example, has changed from meaning *foolish*, to *exact*, to its current meaning of *agreeable* (semantic change).

The organization of whole texts changes too. For example, partly in response to the new technologies used to produce printed language, the conventions which a trainee secretary would be taught to use for the layout of a letter today differ from those in use 30 years ago. The spoken language perceived as appropriate for a conversation between a young woman and a young man who have just met will not only vary according to a range of aspects of the social context, but it will also be different today from what it would have been in the previous century.

Are all these changes inevitably for the worse? Those who comment on them prescriptively imply that they are. If you reflect on the number of times you have heard or read a criticism of some change in 'modern' uses of language, and compare that with the extent to which you hear language change commended, it will become apparent that, for many people, change implies a threat and is something to be deplored and resisted. The vehemence with which resistence is advocated is indicative, I shall argue, of a more profound sense of threat than the arguments which are often advanced make explicit.

One of the arguments put forward for linguistic conservatism is that communication is impeded by whatever change is being identified and criticized. The quotation from Waterhouse, above, asserts that the language he finds so offensive is 'incomprehensible' to most people. The paradox here, of course, is that if a language became incomprehensible to its users it would become obsolete, ceasing to function as a language, which, by definition, is a means of communication. Those who study language recognize that it is always possible to identify and describe the ways in which language users collaborate to communicate their meanings, even if the grammatical rules involved vary among languages and dialects. In this sense, language neither 'progresses' nor 'decays', and change is in fact inevitable (Aitchison, 1991). A language variety may 'die', ceasing to be used at all, but this is the result of social pressures, something which occurs when other languages with greater social or political prestige become used across an increasing range of circumstances. With approximately 300 million native speakers (Wilkinson, 1995), English is hardly an endangered tongue!

Those who seek to alert others to the dangers inherent in the supposed decline in language use may also advance the view that this decline is symptomatic of a decline in other aspects of social behaviour. The Waterhouse piece implies this connection, linking as it does the language and culture of 'modern man' and 'Neanderthal' (Waterhouse's words) language and society. Furthermore, proponents of these views usually identify the trend as originating among the young, and draw conclusions about failings in young people's schooling. It is demonstrable from sociolinguistic evidence that language change does indeed often show itself first among the younger users of a language. However, the factors which are responsible for linguistic change are varied and influenced by economic and political pressures as well as the age of the language user, so that a simple correlation between language 'decline' and the 'inadequate' teaching of the nation's children is erroneous. It is a seductive connection, though, and one which is frequently expressed:

> TV and films bear some reponsibility for declining standards and the substitution everywhere of obscene language for civilized exchanges. The young – and not so young – believe it is tough and adult to ape the semi-literate, foul-mouthed characters presented to them as heroes . . . But the crux of the problem is the Government's neglect of state education.
>
> *Daily Mirror*, 10 September 1992

Language as social practice is expected to carry a heavy burden, and schools are expected to be instrumental in making the nation's language what the public thinks it ought to be. The particular struggles which have taken place over teaching about the English language will be explored further below, but this extract from the Newbolt Report of 1921 gives an initial indication of how strongly its authors felt about the connections between the English language, social relations and the expectations placed on schools:

> The Elementary School might exert a more permanently humanising influence on its products if it were not for the mistake of some teachers in treating English as . . . a mere subject . . . they have to fight against the powerful influence of evil habits of speech contracted in home and street. The teachers' struggle is thus not with ignorance but with a perverted power . . . the lesson in English is not merely one occasion for the inculcation of knowledge, it is an initiation into the corporate life of man.
>
> Board of Education, 1921: 57–60

This extract exemplifies some of the links between point of view and language choices which were reviewed in Chapter 2 – the lexical field, for example, suggests an epic battle between titans: 'evil', 'perverted power', 'struggle', 'corporate life of man'. Contemporary texts also reflect particular points of view, although the metaphors may have changed. Before looking in detail at the history of teaching about the English language in English schools, it is useful to consider briefly the broader issue of the wide range of perceptions about the purpose of school children's education.

Attitudes to schools and the curriculum

One thing which our perceptions of schools and their purpose have in common with our perceptions of language is the difficulty of establishing a critical distance from something so familiar and taken for granted that it comes to seem natural. Elsewhere in this book, it is suggested that one of the key skills children need to develop as they learn about language is the ability to perceive, think about, talk about and analyse not only the 'real world' things to which language refers but also language itself. When we use language to express ideas, it is easy to concentrate on the content and remain oblivious to the language in which it is expressed. Awareness of language makes it possible to notice the choices made by language users, and can make implicit values and assumptions explicit.

Everyone (except the most severely disabled) uses language in some form and to some degree. Everyone in the UK (except a tiny minority educated at home) has the experience of going to school. For many commentators on the state of the language or the state of schools, the universal character of the two phenomena makes their nature appear self-evident and unproblematic. To those of this view, certain forms of language are inherently 'proper' and 'correct', others inferior and dangerous. Efforts must be made to safeguard the former and keep out the latter. One means of achieving this is by ensuring that schools uphold linguistic order against the threat of linguistic chaos. For these commentators, schooling itself is a straightforward, practical activity, whose purpose is to reproduce in the next generation the knowledge and values held by the respected adults in the community, to maintain social order and oppose the ever-present threat of disorder.

However, on reflection, it is self-evident that education is by no means so simple and unified. Even before the development of the National Curriculum in England, which was a component of the more wide-ranging Education Reform Act, there was little evidence of consensus about what schooling was for or what the curriculum should consist of. Once the process of devising curricula for each subject was set in train by the establishment of working parties, there were struggles and resignations, public objections and ministerial reservations, revisions and opposition and repeated reviews and modifications which affected the whole curriculum.

Alternative views of the purpose of schooling

Why are children sent to school and what should they learn there? The roles which schools have in a society embody tensions between the rights and responsibilities of the individual and those of the community as a collective entity, not forgetting tensions between different interest groups within society. Are children at school because they have a right to knowledge, or because society has a right to educated citizens? Do children have the same human rights as adults and if so why is their attendance at this particular type of institution both compulsory and unremunerated? Are children sent to school to protect them from 'society', or to protect society from them? Is the 'basic skill' of literacy the route to individual self-fulfilment or a required resource in a workforce engaged in the industrial and commercial transactions of contemporary capitalism? And should schools differentiate between different 'types' of children?

Some views, again, see an important role for schooling in maintaining a social order which is otherwise under threat from the forces of change and degeneration. Alternative views emphasize the role of schooling in *bringing about* social change. Historically, it has been argued that various groups should not receive education, particularly in literacy, because such emancipation from ignorance would:

> be prejudicial to their morals and happiness; it would teach them to despise their lot in life . . . Instead of teaching them subordination, it would render them fractious and refractory . . . it would enable them to read seditious pamphlets, vicious books, and publications against Christianity; it would render them insolent to their superiors . . .
>
> Davies Giddy, MP, 1807, quoted in Ottaway, 1953: 61

This kind of justification for excluding 'the other' from education has been applied at various times to slaves and servants, to 'the labouring classes', and to girls and women. In contrast, the same political ends have also inspired advocacy of the opposite means: children of all backgrounds should be educated so that they will learn approved values and attitudes, with schools 'furnishing opportunities for their moral and social training' (Board of Education, 1931: 3), teaching deference to 'their superiors', and teaching the things which are required if they are to carry out their work as adults. In this case, the threat of disorder comes from the ignorance, not the education, of the masses.

Other views of schooling emphasize its role in protecting children 'from evil and corrupt influences' and in 'promoting their physical well-being' (Board of Education, 1931: 11; 3). This paternalistic view, which stresses the obligations of society rather than the rights of children, is epitomized in the Hadow Report of 1931, which asserts: 'What a wise and good parent would desire for his own children, that a nation must desire for all children' (Board of Education, 1931: xxviii).

So-called 'progressive' developments in attitudes to primary education emphasize less the school's role in maintaining social order and more the primacy of the individual child, as exemplified in the Plowden Report (Central Advisory Council for Education, 1967). However, although this report advocates that children should be allowed 'to be themselves and to develop in the way and at the pace appropriate to them,' it also states that a school 'must transmit values and attitudes' (para. 505). With a self-assurance similar to that found in earlier texts, the Plowden Report expects that those who work in schools can set out 'deliberately to devise the right environment for children,' confident that adults can take these decisions about what is 'right' for children on their behalf.

Attempts to deploy the forces of schooling for social change are exemplified by the new subjects which began to appear on the curriculum in the 1960s and 1970s. Initiatives were taken in local authorities or individual schools to pursue the potential of formal education for combating some of the inequalities which characterized society outside school. Teachers, and advisers working in educational support services, developed programmes for the promotion of equal opportunities in school children's experience, from preschool to secondary school. These programmes included teaching materials and approaches designed to raise awareness of gender inequalities, racism and the effects of physical disability, and to counteract some traditional perspectives on history and current affairs through the introduction of peace studies.

However, opposition to such curriculum developments, to 'child-centred' schooling and to 'discovery learning', has never been absent from discussion about primary education in the UK, with a great debate about these (among other educational issues) being opened in the mid-seventies. This debate continued beyond the introduction of the Education Reform Act of 1988 into curriculum reviews and yet more legislation in the early 1990s. A further sense in which this continuing debate polarizes 'them' and 'us' and reveals an impulse to shore up the boundaries of order concerns the role of schooling in the definition of nationhood. Once again, a historical perspective illustrates that this tendency is no novelty: the Newbolt Report on the teaching of English (Board of Education, 1921) sought to unify a divided society in the aftermath of the First World War, particularly by emphasizing the subject of English. English was to be shared as 'the greatest benefit which could be conferred upon any citizen of a great state' and would 'form a new element of national unity, linking together the mental life of all classes' (ibid.: 15). For Kenneth Baker, the Secretary of State for Education who introduced the

National Curriculum, national unity through the curriculum, and particularly through English, was also attractive:

> I see the national curriculum as a way of increasing our social coherence . . . The cohesive role of the national curriculum will provide our society with a greater sense of identity.
>
> Baker, in *The Guardian*, 16 September 1987, quoted in Johnson, 1991

> I am working towards *national agreement* on the aims and objectives of English teaching in schools in order to improve standards . . . We need to equip teachers with a *proper* model of the language to help improve their teaching.
>
> DES Press Notice, 16 January 1987, emphasis added

Propriety, standards, unity throughout the nation: a central role has been demanded of both language and schools in distinguishing 'us' from 'them' and in upholding order against the threat of its collapse. The next section of this chapter examines the most explicit combination of language and schooling, the knowledge about language curriculum, and the contradictory forces which have brought it into being.

Knowledge about language: controversy in the curriculum

As we have seen, English as a curriculum subject has had a particular significance throughout its history: 'since the beginnings of mass public education in England and Wales, the teaching of English has been a focus of keen political interest and political control' (Ball *et al.*, 1990: 47).

Why do children need to be taught about language? What should that teaching be? When in children's school careers should the teaching be introduced? How should children be taught about language? There have consistently been tensions in the answers proposed to these questions, both in government policy and in teachers' practice. To some extent, English language and literature have both had to fight for their places in the curriculum, partly in reaction to the considerable status which attached to the classics. Certain attitudes which evolved in the eighteenth century had a far-reaching influence on beliefs about education, including the notion that grammatical descriptions of English were best derived from Latin, and that written language rather than speech provided the best source of language for study. Various commissions of inquiry have issued reports on aspects of this topic, and debates among teachers and with a wider public have found a forum in professional journals and in the media. Different beliefs about education itself, about language and about the role of English in education have bumped up against each other, and the controversy continues.

The Newbolt Report

In 1919, soon after the end of the First World War, a committee was appointed with the following terms of reference:

To inquire into the position occupied by English (Language and Literature) in the educational system of England, and to advise how its study may best be promoted in schools of all types, . . . regard being had to –
(1) the requirements of a liberal education;
(2) the needs of business, the professions, and public services; and
(3) the relation of English to other studies.

Board of Education, 1921: 1

The report demonstrates many of the currents which have for so long pulled the debate about what children need to learn about language, when, why and how, in a number of different directions. One of the concerns which emerges is that English could and should be used in the attainment of national unity, a civilizing influence on all the nation's children, but especially important as a saviour of those at risk from the 'evil habits of speech contracted in home and street'. When members of the committee considered the vexed question of what should be taught about grammar, they found this to be a subject which was 'hotly debated' and that it was 'difficult to discover a general consensus of opinion among practitioners upon any aspect of the matter' (ibid.: 280). They reviewed evidence from various sources and found that, although grammar had had a 'paramount place' in the curriculum of primary schools in the nineteenth century, it had rapidly declined after 1890, once it was no longer a compulsory subject, 'to the joy of children and teacher' (ibid.: 278). The report takes pains to dismantle two erroneous beliefs about the teaching of grammar. Firstly, it exposes the inappropriateness of using Latin grammar as the model for teaching about the nature of the English language. Secondly, it rehearses the distinction between prescriptive and descriptive grammars, advocating the teaching of descriptive skills and quoting with approval from a contemporary school textbook by Wyld:

A Grammar book does *not* attempt to teach people how they *ought* to speak, but, on the contrary, unless it is a very bad or a very old work, it merely states how, as a matter of fact, certain people *do* speak at the time at which it is written.

Ibid.: 281, original emphasis

The report recognizes many of the difficulties which surround the construction of a syllabus for language study: poor teaching, lack of enthusiasm from both pupils and teachers, and the absence of any demonstrable connection between learning about language and improving one's competence in using it. It was felt that there was a need for further study on the part of linguists in relation to descriptive grammars of English, which would eventually lead to the provision of better textbooks for schools. The report's recommendations were effectively a compromise, seeing the study of language as important but to be kept simple and basic, and to be incorporated into other aspects of work in English.

Of course, the discipline of linguistics, and particularly in this context the description of English, has evolved enormously since the period of the Newbolt Report, but other concerns than these have also influenced the world of education. As the status of English as a school subject became more established, during the middle decades of this century, debate continued about the rationale behind the English language and literature curriculum. Developments in 'child-centred' pedagogies began to influence the teaching of language and literacy, so that greater emphasis was placed on respect for children's existing knowledge of the world and of language, and on their right to personal development. As approaches to the teaching of reading and literature began to emphasize the importance of individual response to stories and other texts, and as one of the functions of writing was perceived to be the creative expression of personal beliefs and attitudes, 'old-fashioned' grammar seemed to have even less of a place in the curriculum. At secondary school level in particular, courses in 'language awareness' became more widespread, often linking an acknowledgement of the linguistic diversity of the school population with pupils' introduction to modern foreign languages. Some primary schools sought to celebrate multilingualism in similar ways, but this was not the traditional grammar teaching which would be demanded by those who were to introduce the National Curriculum.

The Bullock Report

Another milestone in the development of the knowledge about language curriculum is the report of the Committee of Inquiry which was set up in 1972:

> To consider in relation to schools:
> (a) all aspects of teaching the use of English, including reading, writing, and speech;
> (b) how present practice might be improved and the role that initial and in-service training might play;
> (c) to what extent arrangements for monitoring the general level of attainment in these skills can be introduced or improved;
>
> DES, 1975: xxxi

The Committee took it as a principle 'that reading, writing, talking and listening should be treated as a unity', stressing the importance of English as the medium through which all teaching and learning is largely conducted and promoting the notion of 'language across the curriculum'. This report, usually known as the Bullock Report, placed a subsection on 'Language study' within their findings on 'Written language'. The principle conclusion on teaching about language itself was that pupils' progress as writers 'should be supported by specific instruction' in certain features of the language, and that:

> these features should certainly include punctuation, some aspects of usage, the way words are built and the company they keep, and a knowledge of the modest collection of technical terms useful for discussion of language.

They went on:

> We must emphasize, however, that everything depends upon the teacher's judgement and his ability to ensure that what is taught meets the needs of the pupil in his writing. Explicit instruction out of context is in our view of little value.
>
> Ibid.: 172

The Kingman Report

By 1984, the Thatcher government was beginning to set up the apparatus for a number of wide-ranging reforms in education, and it was in this context that Her Majesty's Inspectorate (HMI) began production of a 'series of discussion documents . . . intended as a contribution to the process of developing general agreement about curricular aims and objectives' (DES, 1984, 1986). Foreshadowing the format of the National Curriculum documents which were to follow, the HMI report *English from 5 to 16* outlined aims and principles for English teaching and also suggested objectives for pupils at age 7, 11 and 16. The report recognized the contribution of the Bullock Report, quoting from its description of language learning as 'organic', but nevertheless the language modes were presented separately (as they were to be again in the National Curriculum), and a fourth component appeared – knowledge about language. It was recognized that this might be contentious, but the extent of criticism for this aspect of the report in the responses to it was far greater than the report's authors had anticipated:

> Nothing divided the respondents more than the issue of knowledge about language . . . The growth of a stronger accord might be assisted by an enquiry to focus attention on the matter, with the ultimate object of drawing up recommendations as to what might be taught to intending teachers, to those in post and to pupils in schools.
>
> DES, 1986: 40

Soon after this, the then Secretary of State for Education, Kenneth Baker, announced the setting up of just such an inquiry, under the chairmanship this time of Sir John Kingman. In this report (DES, 1988a) knowledge about language was the key concern, with the terms of reference requiring recommendations about the training of teachers 'to understand how the English language works' as well as 'what, in general terms, pupils need to know about how the English language works'. Just as the earlier booklets by HMI had generated an unanticipated response from the profession, so the establishment of this committee also caused controversy. A collection of articles by those concerned with the teaching of English was published while the committee was sitting, partly as a response to the HMI booklets and 'the damage that had been done in confirming ill-informed prejudice', and to the fact that 'much of the publicity surrounding [the] announcement [of the setting up of the Kingman Committee] dismayed the teaching profession' (West and Jones, 1988: v). In particular, the composition of the committee gave cause for concern, as the article by Rosen contributed to the volume edited by West and Jones illustrates. He states serious reservations about the process by which membership of the committee was decided, speculating that those who did not support the views of the government were 'dropped out of the running':

> The result was a committee which left people agape with incredulity. The collective credentials of the members revealed shocking and obvious omissions. Had you

asked those who played an active part in the field of English teaching they would have come up with a list of those who were *not* asked. The list of members constitutes a calculated insult to the English teaching fraternity.

Rosen, 1988: 2

Both teachers and politicians were surprised by aspects of the report when it appeared in April 1988, however. In addition to the inclusion of the required 'model' of the English language, the report took account of the debates about teaching aspects of English language, and, in much the same vein as Newbolt and Bullock, observed:

> We believe that within English as a subject, pupils need to have their attention drawn to what they are doing and why they are doing it because this is helpful to the development of their language ability. It is important, however, to state that helping pupils to notice what they are doing is a subtle process which requires the teacher to intervene constructively and at an appropriate time.

DES, 1988a: 13

One of the members of the Kingman Committee, Professor Brian Cox, explains why the kind of approach advocated in the report caused yet more controversy:

> The Kingman Report was not well received by right-wing Conservatives because they wanted a return to the traditional teaching of Latinate grammar, and the Report came out firmly against this. Many politicians and journalists were ignorant about problems in the teaching of grammar and about the status of Standard English, and simply desired to reinstate the disciplines of study typical of schoolrooms in the 1930s.

Cox, 1991: 4

The Cox Report

The tussle continued into the establishment of the next committee, the working group which was given the task of devising programmes of study and attainment targets for English within the National Curriculum, this time chaired by ex-Kingman Committee member Brian Cox. Cox's own account of the selection procedure is illuminating. He recalls accusations in the left-wing press that education ministers Kenneth Baker and Angela Rumbold had chosen appointees who would reflect Prime Minister Thatcher's Conservative ideology. He reports that, in his view, the ministers simply did not know enough about the issues to predict the likely outcome of the working group's work: 'The politicians were amateurs, instinctively confident that common sense was sufficient to guide them in making judgments about the professional standing of the interviewees' (ibid.: 6).

The first report which was produced by this working group (DES, 1988b), covering, effectively, Key Stages 1 and 2, devoted one chapter to standard English and one to linguistic terminology, but when the report was published,

Baker's belief that grammar had received insufficient emphasis (see Cox, 1991) was signalled in the 'Proposals of the Secretaries of State' which prefaced the working group's recommendations: 'we believe that the first attainment target in writing should be strengthened to give greater emphasis to pupils' mastery of the grammatical structure of the English language' (DES, 1988b: iv).

As Cox reports, sections of the press took their traditional position: 'A Report telling schools to ignore English teaching in favour of trendy methods has infuriated Mrs Thatcher' (*Mail on Sunday*, 13 November 1988, quoted in Cox, 1991). In the second version of the report, which included proposals for Key Stages 3 and 4, the topic of knowledge about language had a chapter to itself, where some of the complexities of the issues were explored, particularly the problem of planning for teaching, which took account of the distinction between implicit and explicit knowledge of language. This chapter also made reference to the fact that, as recommended by the Kingman Committee, a new initiative had been set up by the government, funded by an education support grant, to provide training for serving teachers in the emerging knowledge about language curriculum. This project was called LINC (Language in the National Curriculum), and over the three years from 1989 to 1992, a national team worked to provide training on in-service courses and to produce a package of materials, to support this training for teachers, which was to have been published by the DES and distributed to schools. In June 1991, the then Schools Minister, Tim Eggar, announced that the materials were not to be published after all, and a ban on publication was imposed which made it impossible for the materials to be published commercially anywhere in the world.

Once again, political controversy brought teaching about language to public notice. Press reports exploited the opportunity to resurrect the legendary duel between 'trendy' educationists, with their complex 'theoretical' approach to language, set against the down-to-earth, common-sense man-in-the-street who knows bad English when he hears it. Typical of the headlines was 'Ministers veto "wacky" grammar teaching guide' (Hymas, 1991). A similar theme recurred in other reports:

> Mr Eggar said the way in which the Government's straightforward idea to improve grammar teaching had been 'captured' by the trendies, turning it into an 'abstract argument between educational theorists', was a salutory lesson. 'It ends up with the basics not being taught to schoolchildren . . .'
>
> Massey, 1991

Several articles about the ban on the LINC materials combined this specific story, portrayed as being about grammar and 'correct' English, with a generalized attack on 'progressive' teaching methods, held to be responsible for a general moral and educational decline. As we have seen, this is a familiar theme, and it has resurfaced with each subsequent revision to the English National Curriculum, often accompanied by nostalgic reminiscence about a bygone golden age:

It is time to stop talking about a return to the quality of education Britain enjoyed before the new English humbugs persuaded the education establishment that trendiness was all. It is time to get on with getting back to quality.

Daily Express, 10 September 1992

Thus a familiar discourse is deployed in the representation of descriptive, contemporary approaches to language education as marginal and dangerous.

Standard English

This kind of presentation of the issues is nowhere more evident than in the debate about the place of standard English in the curriculum. 'Standard' is a slippery word. It has connotations of superiority and often features in the discourse made fashionable during the 1980s where words like 'quality' and 'excellence' lend rhetorical weight to an ideological project. A standard also suggests something fixed and reliable, a benchmark against which other versions of whatever is under consideration may be judged. In the context of education, the image of schooling as a 'journey through the target levels', as a DES (1991) pamphlet has it, links with the use of testing and publishing results as the means of 'raising standards' in a visible way. As we shall see below, in a strictly linguistic definition of the standard form of a language, these connotations have no place, but unfortunately the connotations of a word do not evaporate merely because they are more relevant in certain contexts than others.

Descriptive linguists, as we have seen, are not compelled to make evaluative judgements about different languages or different dialects of the same language:

> if people are communicating effectively with language, then they must be following rules, even if those rules are not universally approved. The role of the linguist is thus analogous to that of the anthropologist who, if asked to describe a particular culture's eating habits, would be expected to do so without expressing a personal opinion as to what they should be like.
>
> Leech *et al.*, 1982: 5

Once again, however, it is the interaction of the social and political with the linguistic dimensions of the issue which has led to misunderstanding and conflict over standard English. The belief that a standard version of English could unite all sections of society, if only everyone could be taught to use it, is a myth with a long history. In 1860, the idea that political conflict could be reduced via a standardizing of English was articulated by Marsh:

> It is evident . . . that unity of speech is essential to the unity of a people. Community of language is a stronger bond than identity of religion or government, and contemporaneous nations of one speech, however formally separated by differences of creed or political organization, are essentially one in culture, one in tendency, one in influence.
>
> Quoted in Crowley, 1989: 221

The same notion resurfaces in the Newbolt Report, which expressed the aspiration that the English would, with adequate teaching of 'good speech', become prouder of and more affectionate towards their own language, learning to see its 'maltreatment' or 'debasement' as an outrage: 'Such a feeling for our own native language would be a bond of union between classes, and would beget the right kind of national pride' (Board of Education, 1921: 22).

That these hopes have not met with complete success as the century nears its close is demonstrated by the repetition of similar sentiments by successive government ministers (not to mention Prince Charles), and by the increasing emphasis placed on teaching standard English as the English National Curriculum has been revised. Although it has gone through various stages, the debate has basically been between two positions. One position, held mainly by linguists and educationists, argues that standard English, while it has greater social prestige than other varieties, is not intrinsically superior to them. These writers have also pointed out the difference between spoken and written language, and the fact that, since we do not currently have a full description of the structures of spontaneous speech, although we can identify many of its features, the concept of teaching children to *speak* standard English raises some particular problems. Such writers have also alerted their readers to the common confusion between received pronunciation, which is an accent associated with social privilege, and standard English, which could, at least theoretically, be read aloud in any accent, including very broad regional ones. Despite the way the controversy is usually reported in the press, this position never denies that standard English is a vital component of pupils' social and linguistic repertoire. As the Kingman Committee reported: 'one of the schools' duties is to enable children to acquire Standard English, which is their right. This is not a matter of controversy: no item of evidence received by the Committee contained disagreement with this point' (DES, 1988a: 14).

On the other side of the debate are those whose belief in the importance of standard English leads them to recommend legislation making it compulsory. Some journalists have no problems with labelling non-standard English as inferior, reproducing the connection made in the Newbolt Report, with its references to 'bad English' and concomitant 'bad habits of thought'. In contrast, more recent government reports on the issue have included at least a nod in the direction of recognition that regional dialects should not be devalued. For Kingman, they are 'a source of richness' (DES, 1988a: 14). In the first Cox Report, teachers are advised to teach standard English 'in ways which do not denigrate the non-standard dialects spoken by many children' (DES, 1988b: 15), and this approach underpinned the first version of the English National Curriculum. However, a decision was taken to revise the Order, and to place greater emphasis on not only the written but also the spoken form of standard English. In the first set of proposals for the revision, published in April 1993, the bald and linguistically inaccurate definition of standard English announced that it is 'characterized by the *correct* use of vocabulary and grammar' (DFE, 1993: 9, emphasis added). Since that document was published, the definitions of and requirements for teaching standard English have undergone several revisions, but the notion of 'correctness' and adherence to rules has remained.

What is standard English? As we have seen, linguists are able to describe the rules and conventions which govern the grammar of any language variety, and to demonstrate that none is intrinsically superior to others as a system for conveying meanings. The standard variety does, however, become more fully elaborated, and is able to serve a wider variety of communicative purposes. (On the other hand, some of the features which are retained in non-standard varieties of English allow for greater precision of meaning than is possible in the standard variety. For example, standard English uses *you* as the second person pronoun in both the singular and the plural, whereas some dialects retain *youse* in addition, a distinction which can prevent potential ambiguities (see Milroy, 1984).)

Attempts to define standard English are usually rather circular. They are unable to specify all the grammatical and lexical features which distinguish it from other varieties, as this would take a whole book, and would in any case need constant updating. The catch-all which is usually used to get round this problem is to say that standard English is the variety which English speakers recognize as the standard. One example from a dictionary illustrates the circularity:

1 the English taught in schools;
2 English that is current, reputable, and national;
3 the English that with respect to spelling, grammar, pronunciation, and vocabulary is substantially uniform though not devoid of regional differences, that is well-established by usage in the formal and informal speech and writing of the educated, and that is widely recognized as acceptable wherever English is spoken and understood;
4 all words entered in a general English language dictionary that are not restricted by a label (as *slang, dial, obs, biol, Scot*).

Webster's Third New International Dictionary, quoted in
Quirk and Stein, 1990: 121

It is clear from such definitions that we are dealing with a social, rather than a linguistic, phenomenon. Categories such as those used by 'the educated' and 'widely recognized as acceptable' are social statements.

The situation is further complicated if we take into account the variety and flexibility of language as it occurs in real social interactions. The diversity of such naturally occurring language then pulls away from the notion of a homogeneous standard. Wilkinson (1995) points out that many legal texts, for example, while written in syntactically and lexically 'standard' language, pose considerable challenges of interpretation for the reader. Another text may be informal in style and yet contain no 'non-standard' features. A third piece might seem intimidatingly formal and yet on analysis it may be seen to contain syntactical anomalies. As Wilkinson summarizes (ibid.: 103), 'Standard English . . . can be seen as containing many varieties, which overlap and change according to the nature and audience of the situation. It is a flexible, and constantly changing, vehicle.' Furthermore, standard English – or standard Englishes – share a substantial common ground with other varieties of English. Many features of lexis and syntax are to be found both in standard and

non-standard varieties, and many speakers select differently from their repertoire according to the social context.

Researchers who study the dialects of English are able to supply extensive
evidence of the wide variations in vocabulary and syntax to be found in different regional varieties of English, not to mention the many 'Englishes' which
are developing beyond the British Isles, and are also able to trace some of the
historical journeys made by features in the different varieties which account
for their contemporary use in different areas (see, for example, Milroy and
Milroy, 1993). Such analyses take whole volumes to detail the differences and
their origins, but the government policy documents on the English National
Curriculum confine themselves to a very brief indication of their concerns,
with minimal linguistic detail. Specified in the 1995 version are, 'rules and
conventions of grammar', glossed as 'grammatical features . . . [including] how
pronouns, adverbs and adjectives should be used and how negatives, questions
and verb tenses should be formed' (DFE, 1995: 3). These items hint at the
non-standard features which often cause the most offence to those who feel
strongly about this issue, and coincide largely with the features which linguists
have identified as shared by many urban dialects (Hughes and Trudgill, 1987;
Milroy and Milroy, 1993). Sociolinguistic studies have often found that urban
dialects are more stigmatized than rural ones, and 'non-standard' varieties may
suggest characteristics of their users' class backgrounds as well as their identification with a particular region. In the light of this, we can guess at the usages
with which the 1995 English National Curriculum is concerned. Below are
some examples of the features which pupils are required to recognize to meet
the requirements of this piece of legislation.

Pronouns

This category is presumably included to guard against usages such as *hisself*
and *theirself*, the use of *what* where the standard construction would use *who* or
which, and the addition of *-s(e)* to *you* to mark the plural form, which features
in some dialects.

Adverbs and adjectives

Some non-standard forms of English do not add *-ly* to adjectives to create
adverbs, so that to meet these requirements children would need to learn to
write – and say – *She talks properly* as opposed to *She talks proper* and *He did
that quickly* rather than *He did that quick*.

Negatives

Variations in the formation of negatives are a constant source of irritation to
many people. These include double or multiple negation such as *There wasn't
no money left*, a construction common in earlier English literature as a marker

of emphasis. Two other bugbears are the use of *never* as past tense negator, as in *He did it once but he never [did it] this morning* instead of *He didn't [do it] this morning*, and the use of *ain't* instead of *is not* or *has/have not*.

Questions

It is difficult to infer what is meant by this item, as the formation of interrogatives is not usually included in accounts of the common features of non-standard English. Perhaps the authors are thinking of tag questions, such as *innit?*, as a contraction of the informal *isn't it?*, which can also be formulated as *is it not?* Or perhaps they are concerned about the interrogative construction which omits the second person pronoun and the auxiliary verb *do*, as in *Want some?* rather than *Do you want some?* However, it is debatable whether these are non-standard constructions as opposed to standard constructions as produced in the context of informal speech.

Verb tenses

The main feature of verbs which varies between different dialects of English in the present tense is the addition of the *-s* ending, added in standard English only to the third person singular of regular verbs (excluding the modals *will*, *would*, *can*, *could*, *shall*, *should*, *must*, *might* and *may*, as well as *ought*). In some non-standard varieties, *-s* is added to the first person also, as in *I goes there when I wants to*, while conversely it may be omitted even from the third person form in others, as in *he go*. It is this kind of construction which involves 'agreement' or 'concord' between the subject and the verb, another topic which features throughout the requirements of the English National Curriculum. In other words, the form of the verb is related to the nature of its subject, but different varieties of English show this 'agreement' in different ways. It is meaningless to say that any of these ways is more correct than the others, as comparisons with both other languages and earlier forms of standard English will show. The only sense in which the standard way is 'better' is that it carries social prestige.

It is often observed of young children learning to speak English that they seem to over-generalize the rule which they have inferred about the grammar of the language that to form a past tense *-ed* must be added. This is held to account for constructions such as *Our teacher teached us*, where standard English uses *taught*. A challenge for teachers trying to implement the National Curriculum is that this is both a developmental stage which standard English speakers go through and also a stigmatized non-standard usage in some parts of the UK. English verbs which do not conform to the *-ed* pattern of the past tense, known as 'strong' verbs, have different forms for different functions in a clause, but there are variations within this pattern. Harris (1993: 152) gives these examples of the three patterns to be found in standard English of basic stem, past tense and past participle:

(1) do/did/done, give/gave/given;
(2) come/came/come, buy/bought/bought;
(3) hit/hit/hit, put/put/put.

If you think of the way in which non-standard varieties with which you are familiar form the past tense of verbs, you will probably recall patterns which allow a different form to be used in past tense constructions from the one which is used in standard English. Examples would include *She come here twice*; *I done that*; *They've took it*; *She's wrote her story*. Another past tense irritant is the use of *ain't* in constructions which use *have*, such as *We ain't done that yet*, which has already been addressed under 'Negatives'.

The verb *to be* has the characteristics of being very common, very irregular and, not surprisingly, used differently in different dialects. The issue of subject–verb 'agreement' arises again in the non-standard *we was* and *I were*, and, again, *ain't* is found instead of *isn't* in some dialects.

It is interesting that when social attitudes towards dialect are discussed, it is usually differences in vocabulary which are cited as a 'source of richness', valued as quaint and worthy of preservation, while grammatical markers of variation such as those outlined here are severely stigmatized. This difference may be important for teaching, since evidence about language acquisition suggests that it is vocabulary which is more susceptible to conscious learning, while the rules of the grammar of a child's first language, learned unconsciously, are more deeply embedded and in that sense less 'available' for children to alter (see Chomsky, 1988). A further difficulty which arises from the National Curriculum prescriptions echoes the problem outlined in Chapter 1, that it is not clear what conceptual knowledge is to be included in any teaching. The wording has it that 'pupils should be given opportunities to develop their understanding and use of standard English,' and 'to recognize . . . the grammatical features that distinguish standard English' (DFE 1995: 3), including the items listed and glossed above, but the document does not make clear what is meant by understanding or recognition. It is important to be clear about explicit and implicit teaching and learning about language, but many of the prescriptions in the English National Curriculum blur the distinction. This problem is accentuated by the fact that people do not change their use of language merely because teachers say they should.

Conclusion

In this chapter we have considered the 'complaint tradition', the long-established practice of criticizing a perceived decline in English usage. We have seen how different attitudes towards society and schooling lead to different opinions about what children should be taught about language. Finally, we have looked at the vexed issue of standard English and the details prescribed in the English National Curriculum. Chapter 5 takes up some of the issues raised in this and the previous chapter as we consider the school itself as a linguistic institution.

5 The school as a linguistic institution

Introduction

The previous chapter explored some of the tensions inherent in the process of teaching about language, while in Chapter 2 we considered some of the ways in which available discourses both reflect and reproduce social relationships. We looked at the limitations of a concept of language as a container which transports ideas from the mind of one individual to the mind of another. There are too many variables in social relations and in the potential meanings of texts and utterances for such a simple metaphor to be an adequate description of the role of language in human interaction. This chapter addresses issues related to children's learning about language from the perspective of the school as a social institution, focusing in particular on the part played by language as discourse in the characteristics and maintenance of that institution. We shall look at what children learn about language through their participation as actors in the spoken and written texts generated by the various relationships which constitute the school itself. The chapter begins by considering the range of written texts which relate to the school, and the relationship of these to children's developing awareness of and knowledge about language. Written language is often thought of as superior to speech, and schools obviously have a big investment in the promotion of literacy, but far more words are exchanged through the spoken medium in the course of a school day, and the spoken language encountered and produced by children should not be overlooked.

Written texts and the school

We tend to think of the written texts which children encounter in schools as being the books they read and the writing they do – largely stories, accounts and descriptions relating to various aspects of the curriculum. This can lead to an assumption that it is these texts, associated with the official curriculum, which are likely to be the source of children's data about written language, from which their knowledge about language develops. In fact, the texts generated by the institution of the primary school are far more diverse than this, and even if many of the written texts associated with the school are not primarily intended for children to read, they all contribute to the literacy environment in which the children spend a significant proportion of their time.

How would you classify the range of written texts which are to be found in a typical primary school? Let us imagine a hypothetical primary school and regard it as a kind of case study of written discourses. While the commentary provided below on the texts chosen is not aimed at primary children, it is consistent with the approach to teaching about language which is presented throughout this book, and may help you to experience yourself the ways of conceptualizing language which I am advocating as being helpful for children.

In this composite primary school, in addition to the books aimed at a child audience, there are public texts in the form of notices and announcements, texts which identify people and places in the school, captions to wall displays of children's work, and texts aimed at parents, with the function of seeking help or advertising various school activities. One very public text in this category is the noticeboard at the school entrance which announces the identity and status of the school, accompanied by other details, including the name and qualifications of the head teacher. Less visible to the outsider are the wide range of documents addressed to teachers, such as school-produced policy documents and directives about teaching and the curriculum produced by agencies of central government and the local education authority. Individual teachers have written texts of their own, including schemes of work, which, as well as being shown to senior colleagues, are being redrafted for the external audience of the inspectors from OFSTED who are about to visit the school. The teachers also make use of their own lesson notes, which are far more transitory and are written only for the 'self'. Children too produce private texts, including notes to each other which are intended to be kept secret from an adult audience. On the staffroom noticeboard are texts advertising professional development courses and texts which serve as a reminder that the teachers are participants in the economic and political relations of the labour market: documents from professional associations and job vacancy bulletins.

There are many texts which are on paper, and many others which are recorded electronically. There are many administrative texts, like registers and lists of those pupils who have and have not paid for a school trip and for the visit of a theatre group to the school. These texts are largely controlled by teachers but children are involved in distributing them, as 'register monitors', and in some their participation is more active, as they sign themselves up for a rota of duties or add their names to lists for involvement in various activities. Schools are written *about* in various kinds of text (including books such as this one), and in our hypothetical school there are specialist newspapers and professional journals. Displayed on a noticeboard is a cutting from the local newspaper which gives an account of a charity fund-raising event in which the school played a part.

Each text has not only a physical location – noticeboard, staffroom coffee table, classroom wall – but also a social context which is related to the function of the text, its author(s) and its intended audience. The readers of the texts are 'positioned' in various ways (see Chapter 2) and particular kinds of meanings are encouraged, although alternative readings are possible. Even the physical characteristics of texts contribute to their meaning and significance. Written texts have a 'materiality'. The paper (or other substance) on which they are written, the non-linguistic signs, such as the glass frame, the careful border pattern drawn around a pupil's story, or the dog-eared corners, all influence the way in which texts are read. In this case, the school name-board, which was once quite imposing, has lost something of its original meaning as the paint has started to peel, so the text itself provides evidence of a shortage of financial resources for the maintenance of the fabric of the school.

The choices available to the writers of each of these texts are constrained in various ways. The school's name-board has to comply with the style of every other board in this local authority, and even if the school were to leave the local education authority it would be obliged to follow certain conventions: the use of bright neon paint or of the headteacher's family nickname would widely be considered as inappropriate for this kind of text. The teachers make use of particular discourses when writing their schemes of work, and are thus not only users of those discourses but also the mouthpieces through which they speak. The same is true in a slightly different way of the unofficial and sometimes illicit notes passed between children.

The many written texts to be found in the school make use of lexis and syntax, as all texts do, to structure meanings in particular ways. The tone and style of the texts to be seen may contribute to an impression of how those with the most power in the school regard the institution itself and the community in which it is situated. There is a 'Welcome' notice prominent in the entrance hall, written in a range of languages, with an implicit message that speakers of languages other than English are not neglected in the school. (A reader with racist views, of course, might construe a different meaning from this text.) Alongside this there is a notice which directs 'visitors' to the school office. Readers have to decide whether they come into the category of 'visitor' or not, a classification which may feel inappropriate to those parents who regard the school as belonging to them. A message with connotations of the wider social world beyond the school boundaries, and the conflicting motives and activities of its inhabitants, is provided by the poster reminding the children of 'Stranger Danger', which, aimed as it is at children, uses rhyme to reinforce its message.

Reproduced below are some extracts from a number of the texts to be found in our hypothetical primary school. The extracts are very short, but probably enough for you to recognize the kind of text from which each one is taken. If you can make a fairly confident guess, this is because your knowledge of the genres to which school texts are likely to belong is quite sound. Try to reflect, as you read each one and make a judgement about it, on how you are able to classify the extract as belonging to a particular genre.

(1) All living things need food, but they do not need all the same things. Animals that live mainly on flesh are called carnivores . . .

(2) Aunt Sarah was all duty; Aunt Harriet all temper and fun. A walk with Aunt Sarah was always a lesson; with Aunt Harriet it was an adventure . . .

(3) The Governors and staff endeavour to create a happy and stimulating environment in which children will grow mentally, physically and spiritually . . .

(4) Copies of the final Orders will be distributed to schools in January 1995 for implementation from August 1995 for 5–14 year olds . . .

(5) Please send an envelope to school clearly marked with Mrs Smith's name and the number of tea towels you require and enclose the correct money . . .

(6) And Dad came down and said go up and get dressed so we did. and when we came down Dad said we will go there on satadays . . .

If you did manage to work out the kind of text from which each extract was taken, you will have been drawing partly on your knowledge of the world, of the kind of content you expect to meet in texts which you already knew were to be found in a primary school. So *context* and *content* would be helpful clues. (Since only the words and punctuation are reproduced, you do not have the material, non-linguistic clues to be seen in the actual handwritten, typed or published texts.) Are there additional, linguistic, features which you may have used, perhaps unconsciously? While we must be wary of generalizing from too little evidence, there are stylistic aspects of these texts which are consistent with many texts of their kind: it is partly because they are representative of familiar discourses that you are able to recognize them. By looking more closely at the extracts from the micro point of view, we may also see more about the macro issues of which they are a part.

Extracts 1 and 2 are taken from books written for children, an information book (Showell, 1975) and a story (Bawden, 1975), respectively. The information book includes many sentences of the type used in the example. The simple present tense with a plural subject characterizes many texts which seek to generalize about 'what an entire class of things is like' (Martin, 1989: 15). Some contemporary writers on the learning of literacy in schools, including Martin, are concerned about the limited opportunities offered to children for engagement with this kind of genre, a point to which we shall return below.

Although Extract 2 is also taken from a school library book, it has a more literary feel, and includes an example of the stylistic device known as parallelism. The two aunts are contrasted twice in the four clauses which make up the extract, and an effective balance is achieved by the repetition of the syntactic arrangement of the ideas. From even this very short extract, it is possible to guess at the point of view from which the story is told. The reference to these two characters as 'Aunt', and the description of them in the terms used, positions the reader to perceive them from the point of view of the child who is the central character in the narrative.

The other extract which has an almost literary feel is Extract 3, which is taken from the school prospectus. In addition to the formality of tone achieved by choices of vocabulary like 'endeavour' rather than 'try', the three adverbs which conclude the extract contribute to a rhetorical style in which groups of three are used for their resonant effect. The statutory duty imposed on schools to produce literature which describes the school and its philosophy has a part to play in the shift in the culture of educational institutions in the UK, towards making schools more like commercial enterprises. The voice used in any school prospectus is partly a response to writing for the multiple audiences to whom it is addressed, but similar messages may be conveyed in a more personal style. The prospectus from another school, for example, proclaims, 'We aim for the best for everyone, within a happy, secure environment'. The authors of this text have opted to use the first person, unlike those in Extract 3, where greater formality has been achieved by use of the third person, 'The Governors and staff'.

Authorship of official documents is often concealed, and Extract 4 is a case in point. It is taken from the covering sheet attached to the version of the National Curriculum Orders sent to all schools in England in late 1994 as 'advance information on the Orders' which were to follow in a final version shortly afterwards. There are no personal pronouns in the extract reproduced, and in fact there are hardly any in the whole of the cover sheet. 'Schools' are personalized in a sentence which gives permission for the use of the document for planning, as it is stated that they can do this 'if they wish', and the word *you* is used once when readers are told what to do, 'if you have any queries'. Otherwise, the impersonal tone is maintained throughout the text, which, like the many documents which have preceded it from the same or equivalent sources, has a very authoritative style. In the extract given here, there is an example of the use of the passive, 'Copies . . . will be distributed', with no mention of the agent who will do the distributing, and of nominalization, 'for implementation'. An alternative formulation of the same message would be 'teachers will implement' or even 'you will implement', but such dialogic constructions are very rare in documents of this type.

Extract 5 is from a letter sent to parents via their children, who customarily act as messengers for this kind of text. The softener 'please' precedes a direct-ive written in a quite precise and rather formal style, marked by the choice of 'enclose' and 'require', while the challenges faced by the busy school secretary are evoked by the request for accuracy in the transaction on the part of the reader, 'clearly marked', 'correct'. What sort of spoken language might be used by the secretary in person to a child whose parents have not followed this directive?

The final extract was written by a child, and demonstrates among other things some aspects of written language which the child has yet to learn. The syntax is standard English, but the author has used the simple connective *and* several times, rather than choosing more sophisticated ways of linking events, with the exception of the subordinate clause, 'when we came down'. Most of the orthography is also standard, but the author is not yet fully confident in the conventional use of capital letters. The text in full is in a typical narrative genre, which takes us back to the question of the range of written language which children themselves meet in school, the topic of the next section.

It is unlikely that you would choose this particular set of texts to use with your pupils, but the activity has potential for drawing readers' attention to the knowledge about the world which we bring to even the slightest encounters with texts from familiar genres. The commentary included here may or may not have made explicit aspects of your own knowledge of how you interpreted the different extracts, but there are many features of language to be noticed in any text we come across, and you might try giving your pupils a different range of extracts to explore. Their discussions will be revealing about the clues they use to guess at the texts from which you have taken extracts, and may therefore help in your assessment of what they know about language and how they use that knowledge. Notice also how much knowledge of the macro dimensions of discourse they bring to bear on such an activity, since, as we have seen, the choice of micro elements in any text are partly a realization of its wider social function.

The written language of the official curriculum

In the context of learning about the different subjects which constitute the formal taught curriculum, primary school children have to read texts whose content is about many different things. Research suggests that, because children learn to speak before they learn to handle written language, these texts are more accessible if the vocabulary and syntax used resonate with the kind of language which is familiar from speech. Readers use many different strategies to make sense of print: phonic clues to decode the sounds from the letters, semantic and syntactic clues to predict likely meanings and word order, memory of whole shapes in recognizing words, and contextual clues, which also draw on knowledge of the world. However, especially for children who are not yet fluent and independent readers, extracting meaning from a text may be too great a challenge if the language is too different from spoken language. Perera (1982a, 1982b) gives details of some of the lexical and syntactic features of school texts which cause difficulty for inexperienced readers. She highlights unfamiliar vocabulary and words which have a general, everyday meaning as well as a specialized, technical meaning: *body* as used in scientific discourse to mean any physical entity is a case in point. She also cites, at sentence level, structures which are unusual in speech, such as 'When in battle, the knights wore red tunics over the armour' (1982b: 123), and other examples of the dense structure which characterizes sophisticated written language. The familiar genre of the narrative, which occurs frequently in speech and makes up a large proportion of children's early reading and writing, presents fewer problems than the non-narrative discourses used in the information texts which support the various curriculum subjects. Perera points out that, whereas the chronology of a narrative provides an easily understood structure, factual prose uses different patterns:

> A paragraph may consist of a generalized statement, followed by detailed examples given as evidence of the truth of the first statement; or there may be several apparently disparate examples strung together to be followed by a concluding statement which draws out the similarity between each of the earlier cases; the writer may put forward one point of view and then turn round and put the opposite point of view; or he may give a series of facts, following each with his own opinion or interpretation; and so on.
>
> Perera, 1982b: 130–1

Perera gives advice to teachers seeking to assess the comprehensibility of the texts they use in their teaching of different subjects, but she does not advocate shielding children from the difficulties. Two strategies are suggested to teachers for dealing with this kind of problem, in addition to raising their own awareness of the linguistic issues which it exposes. The first is to consider the possibilities for drawing children's attention explicitly to the features used in these texts, especially if they occur often because of a particular writer's style. The second is to read non-fiction aloud to children in the same way that stories are read aloud, offering a bridge between spoken and written language. The notion of making language visible and exploring it explicitly will be familiar to readers of this book by now, and Chapters 6 and 7 give further suggestions about ways in which teachers can support pupils in thinking about the challenges presented to them in their talking, reading and writing. Investigations of the properties of non-fiction writing are a valuable component of learning about language.

The other side of the coin is the development of children's own efforts to write in an ever-widening range of styles and genres. This is something which has received increasing attention in recent years, and in a particularly marked form in Australia, where the teaching of genres has generated some controversy. The matter of different written genres draws attention to those aspects of the teaching of writing in primary schools which have potential for developing children's knowledge about language. As we saw above, when teachers choose texts for children to read, they have to balance two considerations. On the one hand, there is the need to ensure that a text is not inaccessible because of its distinctiveness from familiar, spoken language and narrative structures. On the other hand, there is the need to ensure that children gradually acquire enough experience of sophisticated written prose to be able to read texts in many different styles and genres. Where children are themselves producing writing, there is a danger that if teachers concentrate on celebrating pupils' abilities as writers of personal, narrative texts, they will not encourage them to learn more about 'factual' writing. The ways in which children are conceptualized, and the discursive constructions of childhood itself, have in the past led

to an emphasis in schools on setting more of those writing tasks deemed to be
fit for children, most obviously personal accounts and stories. This has meant
that teachers have traditionally provided relatively few opportunities for children to experiment with writing arguments, reports, explanations, and so on.
Martin (1989: 57) expresses his disapproval of this danger in avowedly pro-
vocative terms:

> . . . children are the least powerful group of people in our community. And the
> kinds of writing schools encourage them to do reflects this powerlessness . . .
> Unconsciously, the education system has developed a way of not teaching chil-
> dren to write that helps keep them as powerless as possible.

For some theorists, including Martin, the implication of this is that children
should be taught explicitly about the structure of written genres such as the
report, and be given guidance about how to reproduce this structure in their
own work. Critics of Martin's position see the teaching which is advocated as
very teacher-centred, encouraging a misplaced emphasis on 'a formulaic cognitive and linguistic structure' (Stratta and Dixon, 1992: 21). While these
critics agree that pupils should be encouraged to widen their writing repertoire, they are not convinced that 'genres', and the approach to teaching them
advocated by Martin and others, work in the way it is claimed they do. The
'genre' approach is attacked for *dis*empowering children in its failure to allow
for their own priorities and decisions about how, for example, reports might be
written.

Some research suggests that children's ability to deploy the features of prose
increases even without explicit instruction. Perera (1990), for example, points
to the importance of a varied reading diet and opportunities 'to write con-
tinuous passages from an early age', and she also reiterates the usefulness for
learning about writing, as well as reading, of hearing non-fiction read aloud.
So, breadth of experience with different written genres is widely acknowledged
as important, but there is less consensus about teaching strategies.

In the next two chapters, we shall consider how 'models' of successful texts
may be used to support apprentice writers, not as prescriptive formulae but as
data to be examined and learned from. The pedagogical controversies embod-
ied in the 'genre debate' are not confined to written texts, however, and it is
the spoken discourses associated with schools and classrooms to which we now
turn.

School talk

This section concentrates on the spoken language in schools which is produced
in classrooms by teachers and pupils, partly because it is this discourse which
has been most thoroughly studied, but we should not forget that a large part
of the spoken language generated in the course of a school day is not of this
sort. Children talk to other children, and talk differently to their best friend,
their little brother and the child in an older class who is also their nextdoor

neighbour. They talk to the dinner supervisors, who talk to teachers, who talk to each other and to the caretaker. The functions of these different discourses are similar and different in various ways. There are also some similarities, but many differences, between the speech used by the headteacher to the whole school in assembly and that used with a parent who visits for a private inter-view. Like the written texts discussed above, these spoken texts are data which children can investigate in learning about language.

Differences between school discourses and the spoken language which is familiar to children from their experiences in the home have been recognized for some time, although they have been analysed from different points of view. Earlier work took the discourse of the school for granted, and concentrated on the supposed gap between that, as a given standard, and the shortcomings of the children from working-class families whose language was held to be signi-ficantly different from it. A belief in the linguistic deprivation of children from socially disadvantaged backgrounds gained ground among teachers, influenced by the work of educational psychologists. Programmes in the United States, for example, were designed to deal with 'the hypothesis that the deprived child's verbal weakness is so overwhelming that it blinds one to his more subtle but basic deficiency. This deficiency is the lack of a symbolic system for think-ing' (Blank and Solomon, 1972: 178). Note the lexical field used in this brief extract, with its connotations of ill health: 'deprived', 'weakness', 'blinds', 'de-ficiency', 'lack'. Similar beliefs influenced teacher training in the UK. Joan Tough, for example, interpreted classroom dialogues she conducted as illustra-tions of 'the difficulty that many children have in taking part in conversation' (Tough, 1977, cited in Tizard et al., 1988: 5).

Research continued and as linguists and sociologists explored the apparent mismatch between the language of school and home, starting from different assumptions, it began to be recognized that the notion of widespread cognitive and linguistic deficiencies among working-class children was far from accurate. When social and institutional relationships were considered, as well as indi-vidual psychologies, it was possible to see that different approaches to manag-ing social interactions might account for children's different linguistic behaviour. Two major studies of children's language development (Tizard and Hughes, 1984; Wells, 1987) draw attention to the differences between the linguistic potential of home and school. One finding of the former study stressed that it was the different social arrangements of home and school to which children responded by 'behaving differently themselves' (Tizard and Hughes, 1984: 236). It was not that the children were incapable of conversational strategies, but that they were sensitive to the constraints of institutional discourse.

The Bristol Language Project, an extensive longitudinal study into the language development of children from different backgrounds, also followed them from the home into their primary schools and found that:

compared with homes, schools are not providing an environment that fosters language development. For no child [in this survey] was the language experience of the classroom richer than that of the home – not even for those believed to be 'linguistically deprived'.

Wells, 1987: 87

So there are linguistic differences between the two environments, but these may be more usefully thought of as social, cultural and functional differences than as deficiencies within individual children. Two functions in particular are salient in the consideration of classroom discourses, the management and control of large numbers of children by a small number of adults, and the deployment of language in the process of teaching and learning. It is important for teachers to be consciously aware of both these dimensions of school discourse. It is also important to recognize that they are specific and limited language functions which can impose constraints on the potential for children to explore and experiment with the many other discourses about which they are entitled to learn.

The socializing function of school discourse

At other points in this book, I have referred to the advantages of making the familiar strange, of finding ways to achieve a critical distance from language, in order to scrutinize the medium as well as the message, and of appreciating that the familiar world of the school, likewise, is socially constructed and not inevitable. In his book on 'the ecology of written language', Barton (1994: 177) advocates trying to see schools as 'strange, not as normal'. To this end, he describes the practices of the school as they might seem to an outsider, considering the role of language in maintaining those practices:

> There are all sorts of practices which children are learning in schools: children are learning to conform, to be part of large groups, to sit still, to be regulated by time. Schools have their own ground rules of what you are allowed to do and what not, including rules about who may talk, when, to whom, and what about. These ground rules are different from those of home and community. There are many ways in which schools socialize children by the organization of day-to-day rhythms of schooling; language use is a central part of this.
>
> Barton, 1994: 179

Another researcher who has explored the socializing function of language in primary school children's experience is Willes (1983). She provides a detailed account of the processes by which children at the start of their school careers (in nursery and reception classes) are socialized into pupils, and she places considerable emphasis on the functions of discourse in the socialization process. She also draws attention to the way in which linguistic and pedagogic possibilities are constrained by the requirement that the teacher must 'control a number of pupils so as to ensure the safety of each of them', so that 'learning to be a pupil involves learning to participate in the expected ways' (p. 147).

It is tempting to deplore the authoritarianism of the classroom situation in which children's curiosity, creativity and individuality are stifled by a regime which insists on an adult definition of what is important, and which reinforces adult 'rules about who may talk, when, to whom, and what about'. However, it would be naive to suppose that there is infinite scope for the full expression of children's differing needs and interests, given that schools are charged with the social responsibility for keeping children on the premises for specified periods of time and for prescribed purposes, whether they choose to be there or not. It is equally naive to imagine that this structural relationship will not be a key factor in defining the nature of classroom discourse and in constraining the roles of the participants in it. Willes' meticulous analysis (1983) of her reception classroom data reveals the power relationships which structured the discourse: 'The teacher . . . took the initiatives, decided the topics, and remained all the time in control. *Her* consciousness of the kind of discourse proper to the classroom went a very long way towards creating and sustaining it' (p. 122, original emphasis).

Other studies of classroom discourse, in other phases of schooling, have observed the connection between the responsibility of teachers for 'classroom control' and for children's learning, manifest in the kinds of language they use. Barnes (1986), for example, makes these links explicitly when he says, in connection with the language of secondary school classrooms:

> Classroom control is not a matter of reprimand and punishment: these only become necessary when control has broken down. Control is a matter of inducing pupils to give their serious attention to the matter in hand . . . control and the teaching of subject-matter are normally one and the same thing.
>
> Barnes, 1986: 59

Teachers' discourse, then, may be a blend of control and instruction. Their questions have been analysed from the point of view of both functions. Teachers may use questions to which children know they must respond in a formulaic way. For instance, imagine a child has excused some piece of unacceptable behaviour by telling her teacher that another child told her to do it. The teacher replies, 'If Michelle told you to go and jump off a cliff would you do it?' This has the form of a question, but its pragmatic purpose is to position the child, when she supplies the only acceptable response, as being in the wrong, thus confirming the authority of the teacher.

Sometimes children in school exploit the potential for utterances to mean, or signify, something other than the meaning intended by the speaker. Teachers who use rhetorical questions as a means of establishing their classroom authority can find it undermined by children who choose to interpret the question as a genuine inquiry and offer an answer. Conversely, children may find that the dominant discourse which sanctions teachers' questions for purposes of both control and teaching makes it difficult for them to ask their own questions. In relation to her observations from the primary classrooms in her study, Willes writes:

> It is almost impossible for a pupil to ask a question about the relevance of items to each other, or about the evidence for a claim, or about what would be the

prerequisites of understanding a particular matter, without seeming to challenge very directly the teacher's personal authority.

Willes, 1983: 142

These connections between the salient functions of classroom discourse, identified above as control, or socialization, and its pedagogical function, lead us to a consideration of the language used in teaching and learning.

Pedagogical discourse

Some early research into the way teachers speak to children in schools was conducted in secondary classrooms, and it drew attention to a pervasive routine in which the teacher asks a question, a pupil answers the question, and the teacher evaluates the pupil's response (see Sinclair and Coulthard, 1975). This has been labelled the 'IRF' sequence (Initiation, Response, Feedback), characteristic of a discourse environment in which teachers talk more than pupils, and limit the discursive roles which are available to them through tightly structured sequences of question and answer. An example from Coulthard (1977) is cited in Meighan (1986: 158):

Teacher: Those letters have special names. Do you know what it is? What is one name that we give to these letters?   (Initiation)
Pupil: Vowels.   (Response)
Teacher: They're vowels, aren't they?   (Feedback)
Teacher: Do you think you could say that sentence without having the vowels in it?   (Initiation)

The limitations of this kind of discourse for effective learning have long been recognized, leading to repeated criticisms of this style of teacher talk. However, it may be regarded as assessment rather than teaching, an indication for the teacher of whether pupils have learned specific items of information. Or its function may, as described above, be more relevant to control than to teaching. If so, children are likely to be learning from exchanges like this something about these functions of discourse as well as about the subject on the timetable.

These considerations are not confined to secondary school classrooms, and primary teachers will recognize the IRF sequence. I think it is important to appreciate that teachers are not necessarily to be blamed for making use of the available discourses, and that our ideals for teaching styles which do encourage children to be creative, inquisitive and vocal cannot always be realized. It is very difficult to find oneself positioned as a teacher and *not* make use of the available discourses for 'doing being a teacher'. Many primary teachers are overtly critical of closed questioning, for example. They may also deplore the well documented tendency of teachers to select boys to answer questions more readily than girls (see, for example, Swann, 1989), and would wish to do neither of these things themselves. However, patterns of classroom discourse are not only the responsibility of individual teachers, and sometimes we are not conscious enough of their influence to be in a position to choose to use language differently. Furthermore, since children are also active social beings in the classroom, their expectations of what the discourse should be like will have an influence. Children may be even more committed to 'doing being a pupil' than you are to maintaining your authority and 'doing being a teacher' (see Davies, 1983). One example of this in my own experience comes from a classroom exchange where the well established dynamics of classroom discourse led to a pragmatic misunderstanding. I was showing some children a video of their own class at work and wanted to encourage their observations and comments, and so when one child noticed something on screen and quietly pointed it out to his friend I thought his observation might begin the discussion. My invitation, 'Do you want to say something, Tyrone?' was read as the kind of teacherly reprimand which it often is. It resulted in a chastised look and an apologetic, 'No, Miss'.

If you do want to make changes, or to use classroom discourse as data in your teaching about language, it can be instructive to record yourself teaching, to find out about the discourse of your classroom as it actually is, as opposed to what you think it is like. You can also use school discourses as the basis for scripts which the children devise as a means of exploring how various transactions are executed through language. You can set a scene based in school which involves characters such as pupils, dinner supervisors and teachers, and some kind of conflict, such as different interpretations of behaviour. By improvising and scripting the dialogue, children have the opportunity to make visible aspects of the language which operates in these situations, and to consider alternatives.

The discourse of 'child-centred' pedagogy

There are some additional aspects of the discourse of the primary classroom which derive from the dominant perceptions of what young children are like and how they learn. The central issue here is the ideology of 'child-centred' approaches to education and the attendant notion of 'discovery learning'. There are many good reasons to criticize didactic teaching, which, as discussed above, may teach children to be passive and subservient rather than assertive and articulate, and may be irrelevant to their intellectual needs. In reaction to these traditions, primary school education in the UK has been heavily influenced since the 1960s by the psychological experiments of Piaget, and by the interpretations of his conclusions about how children learn, as expressed in the Plowden Report. Considerable emphasis in this approach to teaching young children is placed on *not* using language as a medium of instruction if there is a danger that the child does not yet have the equivalent experiential knowledge: 'Verbal explanation, in advance of understanding based on experience, may be an obstacle to learning, and children's knowledge of the right words may conceal from teachers their lack of understanding' (Central Advisory Council for Education, 1967: para. 535).

Edwards and Mercer (1987) describe a study of the discourse of primary classrooms in which they found that teachers had been heavily influenced by this perception of children needing to discover things for themselves, rather than being told by teachers. These researchers conclude from their extensive observation of a range of primary school lessons that part of the knowledge of discourse which pupils were having to learn was 'how to play the classroom game', negotiating 'the unspoken and implicit ground-rules of the system'. They found that teachers had specific learning goals in mind but went out of their way not to share these explicitly with their pupils. The result was that: 'For many pupils, learning from teachers must appear to be a mysterious and arbitrarily difficult process, the solution to which may be to try to concentrate on trying to do and say what appears to be expected – a basically "ritual" solution' (Edwards and Mercer, 1987: 168–9).

These authors are also critical of the perception which emerges from Piaget's work of children learning as isolated individuals, rather than as social beings. Teaching which places too much emphasis on the child as lone explorer, finding out as an individual about a complex environment through activities which the teacher has structured and planned but not explicated, is receiving increasing criticism. Edwards and Mercer (1987: 169) found in their study that primary teachers' educational ideology led them to a view of pupils as 'essentially individuals in pursuit of a realization of their own individual potentials'.

This study acknowledges the importance of work carried out by psychologists such as Bruner, who has been very influenced by the writings of Vygotsky. One of Vygotsky's important contributions to understanding the potentials of classroom discourse is his recognition of the social nature of learning. Vygotsky draws attention to the vital role in children's learning of joint activity and conversation with more experienced members of the culture. He also describes the notion of a 'zone of proximal development', where children are able to do with support ('scaffolding') what they would find too challenging to accomplish on their own. According to Edwards and Mercer, these ideas offer the potential for a model of classroom discourse which is like neither traditional, didactic teaching nor the kind of discovery learning in which teachers are inhibited from being explicit about classroom activities. These authors make it clear that they do not wish to criticize those aspects of progressive educational movements which are an argument for 'children's active engagement in their own learning' (ibid.: 36). However, they do identify a 'fundamental dilemma' for teachers. Teachers have to find a way of balancing a 'child-centred' pedagogy, on the one hand, with the need to act as 'society's agents of cultural transmission' (ibid.: 168) on the other, a tension which others have also recognized, as we saw in an earlier section. Edwards and Mercer advocate that, rather than choosing between these two versions of teaching and learning, teachers might consider 'a third step, towards a cultural-communicative model of education' (ibid.: 36). You may remember from Chapter 3 a quotation from Bruner about the communal nature of learning, and the limitations of a view of development which extracts the individual from culture and community. These attempts to depolarize pedagogical controversies have some particular relevance to teaching about language itself, the central concern of this book. In the arguments about 'progressive' primary pedagogy versus 'traditional' teaching methods, there is a tendency for adherents of each position to caricature the views of the other, and this is also true of a number of issues in language teaching. In the teaching of reading, for example, we have witnessed a polarization of 'real books' (a resource) against 'phonics' (a strategy), and of learning orthodox analyses of a canon of great works against celebrating the response of the individual reader. In relation to knowledge about language, a polarization has been constructed which pitches didactic, decontextualized, prescriptive grammar teaching against no teaching about language at all.

McCarthy and Carter (1994) draw attention to similar kinds of polarities in a book about teaching English as a foreign language. Reviewing the different approaches and emphases in teaching language, these authors note 'some familiar contrasts and dualisms creeping into our discourse,' and they list some examples, including 'explicit learning about language v. implicit learning about language,' 'form-focused v. meaning-focused,' 'conscious v. unconscious,' 'language as static v. language as dynamic,' 'accuracy v. fluency,' and so on. Their conclusion, reminiscent of the 'third step' identified by Edwards and Mercer, is that, 'instead of adopting a dualist perspective' it is preferable 'to explore the possibilities of integration of these seemingly opposed theories of language learning' (p. 161).

Conclusion: implications for teaching about language

This chapter has suggested, then, that in relation to both pedagogical discourse in general and to teaching about language in particular, there is room for synthesis and integration of the most useful elements of different approaches. What would this mean for teaching about language in the primary school? What kind of a curriculum for learning about language would be generated? That question will be answered in more detail in the next two chapters, but it is appropriate to give an indication here of the implications of the material discussed in this chapter, which has been a consideration of the school as a linguistic institution.

Firstly, such a curriculum would recognize that the school itself is the source of a rich variety of texts. These texts provide a common pool of knowledge, experience and relationships, which offer the potential for exploring language at both micro and macro levels. However, if school texts and discourses have specific social functions, as they surely do, then their limitations as sources of language to be used as data would also need to be recognized. It follows from this that teachers would need to ensure that children have access to other kinds of texts and discourses from those usually found in schools and classrooms. If children are to learn about different functions for language, they need at best authentic, or at least simulated, experience of social relationships in which the discourse is not that of the classroom, in either its socializing or pedagogic guise. Finally, there is the possibility of making real progress beyond the sterile arguments about traditional versus progressive approaches to teaching about language. The primary school class-room is the product of social forces and relationships which produce and constrain the discourses produced there. There are limits to the ways in which both teachers and pupils can realize their respective positions, but these limits are not inflexible. There is every reason to capitalize on the experience in primary classrooms which demonstrates that the opportunity to carry out their own investigations and to make discoveries for themselves is crucial to children's developing understanding. In addition, we can acknowledge that more experienced language users and members of the culture, including especially teachers themselves, can help children to learn by providing not only guidance but also explicit information and teaching.

6 Teaching about language: principles and methods

Introduction

As we have seen from previous chapters, primary school pupils are social beings who already know a lot about how to use language in practical ways. While they are in school, they inevitably take on aspects of the social role of pupil, just as you, largely through the language you use, take on aspects of 'being a teacher'. This means that the teaching–learning interactions which are possible in the classroom are not the only kinds of knowledge about language to which the children have access, but it is these which constitute the official curriculum, over which you have most control. This chapter begins by considering why primary school teachers should teach about language itself, bearing in mind the various aspects of the context which have been outlined in preceding chapters. It goes on to explore various pedagogical principles which are likely to make teaching about language more successful, including the idea of consciousness raising and the role of literacy in language awareness, the usefulness of collaborative approaches, the central importance of texts rather than exercises in teaching children about language, and of investigative approaches to language study which seek evidence on which to work. The chapter goes on to consider the relevance of classifying data and identifying patterns in language, and the utility of authentic contexts and purposes for learning about language. It concludes by exploring the role of the teacher in planning for teaching about language. The principles and methods for teaching about language presented are illustrated with examples of children demonstrating and developing their knowledge about language. In each case, the areas of knowledge touched on in the examples are referred to in Figure 2.1 (p. 28). This, you may remember, listed the micro elements of phonology and orthography (P/O), lexis (LX), grammar (including morphology, word classes and syntax) (G), and semantics (S), and the macrolinguistic dimensions, when texts are situated in communicative contexts, of language and society (LS), language acquisition (LA), language change (LC), and language varieties (LV).

A rationale for teaching about language

In planning your teaching about language, it is important to have a rationale in your own mind, preferably one which has been discussed with colleagues. This can then serve as a framework when considering the detail of what is to be taught. The first imperative for teaching your pupils about language is that this is now a legal requirement. Earlier chapters have given some indication of the areas of knowledge which are required, although, as we have seen, there are gaps and ambiguities in the policy documents about the detail, and about the sequence in which children are likely to acquire the requisite knowledge. The National Curriculum for English as it is currently constituted does not include a full rationale for teaching about language, but within the texts which together comprise its complex history, various points of view have been put forward. While the rationale implied in later versions of the English National Curriculum places much greater emphasis on 'accuracy', 'appropriateness' and 'correctness', the second Cox Report has several paragraphs about its rationale. The report's more balanced summary includes two specific points. Justifications for teaching pupils about language include:

> first, the positive effect on aspects of [pupils'] use of language and secondly, the general value of such knowledge as an important part of their understanding of their social and cultural environment, since language has vital functions in the life of the individual and of society.
>
> DES, 1989: 6.6

Very little research has been done on how primary children's language competence, their skills and abilities as talkers, readers and writers, are improved by learning about language. Poor teaching about language may if anything be counterproductive, but it is almost inevitable that if teaching encourages children to be interested in language and enables them to feel that it is within their conscious control when they need it to be (which will by no means be all the time) then their achievements as language users will be enhanced.

If children are to become familiar with the significance and nature of standard English, as required by the 1995 Orders, then it is necessary to teach about it and, by definition, about other varieties of English. A critical awareness of the nature of language and the social issues with which it is associated is empowering, enabling children to make more informed choices about their own uses of language and about their responses to those of others. (For further discussions of 'critical language awareness', see Ivanic, 1990; Fairclough, 1992; van Lier, 1995.)

Consciousness raising

We have noted throughout this book that learning *about* language is different from many other areas of the curriculum because linguistic competence does not develop through explicit instruction in the same way that, say, competence with a set of practical tools needs to be taught and learned. Language is so much part of children's routine experience that to 'see' the medium rather than the message can be difficult. Some traditional approaches to teaching about language have dealt with this by bringing aspects of language to children's conscious attention in a rather negative way. The most extreme version of this approach gives children the idea from the outset that there are fixed rules and that the children have probably broken them. The popular series of *Nelson Grammar* books introduces itself as being about 'rules', including the misleading information that, 'Because English is spoken in so many parts of the world, it is important that everyone who uses it should keep to the same rules' (Ballance and Ballance, 1979: 3). In fact, of course, languages diverge as they spread across geographical space and even 'standard' versions of English are not completely identical in, say, Scotland and California. This approach to teaching children about language is understandable in seeking to make familiar examples of language usage visible and available for adjustment. This is probably the motive behind the kinds of exercise where children are presented with sentences containing deliberate errors, for the sole purpose of demonstrating that they know how to 'correct' them. These approaches to teaching about language have been labelled a 'deficiency pedagogy', in that they emphasize what pupils do not know and the 'mistakes' they make rather than capitalizing on the knowledge they already have:

> Pupils lack the necessary knowledge and the gaps should therefore be filled. It is, of course, no accident that gap-filling is one of the main teaching and testing devices associated with such exercises with the teachers fulfilling the role of a kind of linguistic dentist, polishing here and there, straightening out, removing decay, filling gaps and occasionally undertaking a necessary extraction. The deficiency view here is that pupils lack the right language and that such deficiencies or gaps have to be made good.
>
> Carter, 1990: 105

Are there alternative ways of bringing language to children's attention? One way to conceptualize the process is to think less about highlighting mistakes and pitfalls and more about raising the children's consciousness of language and how it is used. 'Consciousness raising' is a term borrowed from the field of second- and foreign-language acquisition. We have already noted that although a first language, if it is learned at the stage when children typically learn their mother tongue, does not need to come to children's conscious attention in order to be mastered, it is often the second language learned which brings language itself, and its rules and conventions, to the level of conscious awareness. The situation is slightly different for that huge proportion of the world's population who experience bilingualism as a norm, but in the UK, with foreign languages usually not taught until secondary school, only a minority of primary school pupils are in the fortunate position of being able to draw on two or more languages for their concept of what language is.

In foreign-language acquisition, the distinction between implicit and explicit knowledge is almost the inverse of the distinction made in relation to knowledge of a first language. For teachers of a foreign language, the movement is likely to be *from* explicit knowledge, a result of teaching about the target language, *towards* implicit knowledge, where the knowledge gained becomes embedded and can be deployed by the learner without conscious effort. In raising young children's consciousness of their first language, the move is rather the other way, bringing to the surface embedded concepts, which are already used without the child necessarily being aware of them. If, however, the learning stops there, it is possible that it will not make any difference to children's language competence, so there is a need for a third stage, in which the newly explicated knowledge may be put to active use in the child's speech or writing. Ellis (1992) suggests a three-part process. Ellis is writing about *second*-language acquisition, which does not rely on pre-existing implicit knowledge of the target language but seeks to bring it about, and the learners are older than primary children, with well developed literacy skills. Nevertheless, the stages identified are useful in thinking about how English-speaking children may become conscious of aspects of English – and this need not mean exclusively 'grammar':

(1) noticing (i.e. the learner becomes conscious of the presence of a linguistic feature in the input, whereas previously she had ignored it).
(2) comparing (i.e. the learner compares the linguistic feature noticed in the input with her own mental grammar, registering to what extent there is a 'gap' between the input and her grammar).
(3) integrating (i.e. the learner integrates a representation of the new linguistic feature into her mental grammar).

Ellis, 1992: 238

This is expressed in rather technical language, so let us take an actual example from the language of a young child to see what it might mean. This short dialogue (reported in Sealey, 1994) took place as a 5-year-old child, Leon, was playing shops with his grandfather, David. He had laid out his wares on the floor – a range of toys and things he had drawn – and instructed David to be the customer:

Leon: You choose one of these to buy from me.
David: I'll have that one there.
Leon: Well, this one isn't very good so you can have this . . .
David: It's imperfect then, isn't it?
Leon: Unperfect.
David: Imperfect.
Leon: Unperfect.
David: Unperfect. Then it's worth even less in that case!

In this exchange, some aspects of what the child knows about language are apparent, others may be inferred and about others we can only speculate. Many words in English do form their antonyms (or opposites) by the addition of the prefix *un-*, and Leon's use of this to form *unperfect* suggests that he had a model of this in his 'mental grammar' (G). He must have 'noticed' that there was a difference between his version and David's, because he attempted to 'correct' David rather than letting David's use of *imperfect* pass unremarked, in which case he would have answered his question rather than focusing on the word he used, and 'comparing' the two versions. What the exchange does not show, and this is unlikely to be seen until some time later with any learner, is whether the discussion and the 'teaching' by the more expert language user led to the stage of 'integration'. This would mean that Leon would know in future, and could use the knowledge, that some words at least take *im-* rather than *un-* to make their antonyms. It is likely that he already had this implicit knowledge from his experience of the word *impossible*, which was in his active vocabulary, but the disagreement about how to form the opposite of *perfect* brought the topic up explicitly, probably for the first time.

The role of literacy in language awareness

The fact that written language does need to be consciously learned is helpful for teachers in that it literally makes visible many aspects of language itself. Sounds are ephemeral. They travel through the air and are gone as soon as they are uttered. Words on a page, however, may be seen and examined, and beginning writers need to think consciously about what they are doing in order to make the language appear – to encode their own meanings into writing or to decode the meanings which have been written down in what they read. Many commentators have observed that experience with written language is critical in triggering children's 'metalinguistic awareness' (see Chapter 3). The very concept of 'word' is much more obvious when words are written down and separated by spaces, in contrast with the strings of sounds which constitute spoken language. Likewise, grapho-phonic correspondence, the relationship between sounds and letters, encourages attention to that aspect of language. Approaches to the teaching of initial literacy which encourage children to experiment with texts, and to behave in the same way as more experienced readers and writers do, take the emphasis away from what they do not know about written language and make use of what they have already learned, while continuing always to increase both conscious knowledge and active competence. This includes knowledge at many levels, from the basic awareness that print conveys meaning, to the conventions of layout in books and other texts, to the precise spellings of individual words. In addition, children are also aware of literacy on the more macro level, and their consciousness of its significance as a social practice does not need to wait until they are expert readers and writers.

These observations about the role of literacy in language awareness are well documented in the literature, although in addition children need opportunities for reflection if they are to realize themselves how their knowledge about language develops through experience of literacy. The following example is just one illustration of how a group of children made some of their perceptions about writing explicit. As part of a project on different aspects of writing, some

Year 6 children recorded, among other things, the reasons why they thought writing was important and the aspect of writing with which they had most difficulty. It was the social significance of writing (LS) which was mentioned most frequently as its importance. Lots of responses mentioned the instrumental value of writing in terms of life chances – 'so you get a good job', 'a lot of jobs involve writing' – but some referred to its relevance for personal status – 'so you have a good reputation'. The practical importance of writing was recognized, both for interpersonal communication – 'to be able to write a letter' – and for individual purposes – 'If you had to stop a lesson you wouldn't be able to record anything and when you came back to it you wouldn't remember what you'd done'; 'you wouldn't be able to put your ideas down on something'. The children implied an awareness of the permanence of writing – 'The world would have no history in the future', 'If we could not write we would not give records for anyone else' – and of the link between reading and writing – 'Your reading would be very bad if you don't write'; 'If you could not write it would be hard to read' (LA). There was mention of the need to be familiar with public print, such as road signs and menus, and of writing as a pleasurable activity, especially in relation to stories. While these were all macro level perceptions of written language, much greater emphasis was placed on micro level concerns when the children completed the sentence: 'The biggest problem I have when it comes to writing is . . .'. Some mentioned basic physical skills: 'that my writing is too light' (i.e. faint). Other problems were neatness, spelling, 'joining my letters', 'mistakes', 'when I forget to put capital letters in' (P/O). A few children wrote about the difficulty of thinking what to write, and of the problem of matching their writing ability to their speed of thinking. All these ideas seemed to be easily accessible to the children when they were prompted to think about them, but the task, which involved explicit reflection, provided an opportunity for them to put these perceptions into words and discuss them.

What else raises children's consciousness of language?

Children's experience of formal instruction in reading and writing cannot fail to make them aware of particular aspects of language, at both the micro level of the details of spelling and punctuation and also the macro level of different kinds of written texts and the social status attached to literacy. There are many other experiences which bring language to their attention. Some of these will be planned and formally set up by teachers, while others are unpredictable, incidental to teaching and learning tasks which may be in other curriculum areas. Recalling Ellis' first stage in consciousness raising of 'noticing', there are various occurrences which cause language to come to children's attention. A fundamental principle in thinking about how this works is that children, like all human beings, expect their experiences to make sense, and will strive hard to find meaning even in confusing or ambiguous messages. Hence the familiar substitution of 'Harold' for 'hallowed' when children learn the Lord's Prayer.

From their experience of what can be a person's name, and if no meaning can be extracted from the archaic 'hallowed', the substitution, although amusing to more expert language users, is consistent with children's meaning-making practice. Thus children may force an unclear message to make sense to them at the expense of accuracy, as sometimes happens when they read. If children's reading experiences have taught them that the texts they read are likely to make sense, then they are more likely to employ the strategy, when confronted with an unfamiliar word, of 'reading' an acceptable alternative. If this happens, it will usually be a grammatically acceptable substitute. Then, if the misread word proves not to be meaningful as the text progresses, children may go back and re-read, a process rather like the unconscious speech repairs we all make when we correct an inaccurate utterance.

However, some breakdowns in meaning bring the linguistic medium to people's attention, particularly if the message cannot be 'repaired' at the subconscious level. In the context of reading aloud to an adult, this is when the child may say (employing metalinguistic terminology, although we do not usually think of it as that) 'What does that word say?' Similarly, when children ask 'What does X mean?' in response to a spoken utterance, they have reached the stage of 'noticing' something about language and there is scope for focusing on language itself. The following was a brief exchange between a parent and a 9-year-old child, in which his interest moved from the meaning of a single word to its derivation and links with a base word or root word (LX, G, S):

Child: Why are Batman and Robin called the dynamic duel?
Parent: Duo. It means two people, together.
Child: Yes, but why are they called the *dynamic* duo?
Parent: Dynamic means exciting, full of action.
Child: Like dynamite, 'cos they're dynamite.

As we have noted, however, it is not only at word level that language comes to the attention of its users, and children are no exception. They notice the import of what people say, as well as its literal meaning, and demonstrate by their responses whether they accept the social meaning implied in what is being said. Where children feel able to challenge such things as tone of voice, which is more likely in peer-group interaction than in dialogue with teachers, they may draw attention to it, as a feature of language, so that this aspect of language itself becomes the focus of comment.

Children's consciousness of the social significance of language is raised by teaching which encourages them to reflect on their own experience of these things. For example, some children in a class of 8–10-year-olds did a short project on talk. They devised questions to form the basis of different groups' investigations, which they put forward, during a whole-class lesson, for the teacher to scribe on the blackboard. Some of these questions revealed awareness of differences in socially acceptable styles of talking in relation to age and social class (LS):

Why can't children speak to everyone in the same way? (I can say 'shut up' to P [another child], but I couldn't say 'shut up' to a relative.)

How come people speak differently to more important people than they do to ordinary people?

Why do posh people talk differently from us?

If a first step to learning about language is having language come to one's conscious attention, then teachers need to be aware of this, and to exploit opportunities when they arise. They can also plan tasks which will include this objective, some examples of which are given in Chapter 7.

Collaboration

Collaboration is another important dimension of teaching about language, especially since consciousness raising involves making explicit what is otherwise implicit. Group work as a feature of primary school pedagogy has been subject to swings of fashion. Some studies have revealed that methods of working which appeared to be collaborative were in fact no more than children working simultaneously at individual tasks while seated in small groups. Teaching which relies on group cooperation may also be criticized for making it easier for children who are readily distracted to do little active learning, and for creating an environment in which there is too much noise for children to achieve sustained individual progress. Rigid adherence to group work as a philosophy may take too little account of individual learning styles. On the other hand, when it is properly managed, with clear educational objectives, the enterprise of working with others provides opportunities for learning which are simply not available to the individual working alone. In relation to learning about language, it may be only through collaboration that children make explicit and raise to their conscious attention aspects of language which, as individual writers, they would deploy unreflectively and possibly less effectively. Children may also need explicit teaching about what collaboration means, including how to divide the task into different areas of responsibility, how to ensure everyone's voice is heard, how to negotiate and reach a consensus or compromise when there is disagreement. The kind of discourse generated in small groups like this is distinctive and may be different from other kinds of talk the children routinely engage in. You may need to explain the difference between being influenced by the people in a group and being influenced by their ideas. It is inevitable that children will have difficulties with things like this, but it is an important learning process.

What kinds of collaboration lead children to become more aware of language? One of the principal ways in which this happens is when children collaborate on the construction of a text. At various stages throughout this process, there is bound to be the need for explicit negotiation about the text, and for individuals to justify their preferences for including particular linguistic material. These are very common features of the process, but we will take one example as an illustration. A group of children from a Year 3 class worked together to produce a report for the governors of their school. The headteacher was in the process of allocating some funds for refurbishment of part of the school site, and he actively encouraged the children to have their say in the decisions about priorities, by finding out what needed most attention, canvassing the views of other children and interviewing various relevant adults, so that they could write a report for presentation to the school's governing body. The following extracts are taken from a dialogue between two girls who had decided to update their section of the draft report to take account of renovation work which had been carried out while the school was closed for a short holiday. By this stage, a lot of basic planning had already been agreed, so the first extract presented here concerns the detail of how to write this particular subsection.

Angie: We could do a little subtitle, like 'What has happened.'
Sarah: 'What has happened during the Easter holiday.'
Angie: Then we could do.
Sarah: Take it in turns to do – we could each do so much – what it's going to do, what's happened.
Angie: 'What improvements have happened during the holidays.'
Sarah: 'What improvements', shall I put 'have been made'?

The attention to language in this extract covers several areas. The children think about the mechanics of getting the writing done, by means of turn taking, and, characteristically of this couple, they make suggestions and check for agreement each time. They think about the layout of the text (T) and the relevance of a subtitle, and they think carefully about the wording, moving from the rather vague 'what has happened', to the more specific and relevant 'what improvements have happened' to a final version in the passive voice: 'What improvements have been made' (G).

The main improvement to the playing area by the school was that the pond had been fenced in, and they wanted to express their approval of the expenditure. They drafted a sentence about the previously unfenced pond, 'which was quite dangerous':

Sarah: which was dangerous.
Angie (writing): I think that's right. It's got a 't' in it, hasn't it?
Sarah: No, that's the witch which flies on a broomstick, Angie. You don't want a witch flying on a broomstick in our report to the school governors, do you?

Here, Sarah remembered the different spellings of *witch* and *which*, and humorously reminded Angie of the distinction, so that it was unnecessary for Angie to consult either a teacher or a dictionary to use the correct spelling (P/O). This exchange also included a reminder of the audience for whom the text was intended, so that Sarah's last observation was at both the micro level of a spelling and at the macro level of the whole text (T). This kind of interplay between micro and macro level concerns is common in children's discussions of language, and makes a model of development which moves in a linear way from the smaller to the larger units of language impossible to sustain.

Recent initiatives on the teaching of writing, such as the National Writing Project, have made it clear that teachers must pay attention to the process of writing and not merely to the finished products, and discussions like those between these two young writers offer an insight into ways in which the process involves explicit knowledge about language. In these circumstances, the text does not appear in a linear unfolding, but is collaboratively constructed and is modified even as the child acting as scribe converts spoken ideas to written language. The occasions when the children have to draw explicitly on their linguistic knowledge are likely to include the planning stages, points at which the draft text is reviewed, and moments of uncertainty, disagreement or breakdown of shared understanding between group members. In the context of collaborative writing, children's awareness of the reader's needs grows through the experience of having their own writing read by others. This powerfully raises their awareness of how written language works.

Texts as models

In order to 'notice' aspects of language as used by accomplished speakers and writers, children need access to examples of texts produced by them, and this is the sense in which I am using the term 'models'. Again, this contrasts with a textbook approach, where the language presented for study is contrived, usually no longer than a single phrase or sentence and often exclusively for the purpose of correcting or gap filling.

Children are likely to have noticed already many of the features which distinguish different kinds of texts, in the course of learning to be literate, but if you want to teach about language itself it is important to provide opportunities for shared perusal of particular examples of different genres and to encourage attention to their linguistic characteristics. Learning about language may often occur at the interface, as it were, between reading and writing, when reading is linked to the production of equivalent texts by the children themselves, rather than using texts to extract meaning without reference to their properties as texts. This kind of process encourages children to empathize with readers, when in the role of writer. In these ways, attention is once again on the medium – language – as well as the message of the text.

In the example of the report for school governors described above, the children were initially presented with examples of authentic documents to read before deciding on a format for their own report (T). They looked at some minutes of governors' meetings, and found the formal language difficult, but they were able to identify some salient features of the style. They said that stories were more interesting to read than reports: 'It's harder concentrating on a report than it is on a story'; 'A story has got funny bits in it.' They compared this kind of report with those they had written after doing science experiments, and with newspaper reports, and debated the differences between these, 'true stories' and fiction: 'Anything can happen in a story but it's all got to be true in a report.' They decided that their report should have different sections for the different recommendations they would make about spending the money. They also felt that they would have to justify their ideas:

> Sarah: We could like argue and say it's not fair because all Year 3 have to share one sink.
> Graham: We're not arguing, we're debating.

They thought that the report should be word-processed, 'because all grown-ups do it on the computer', and decided that there should be diagrams, but not pictures, in the final version. Other texts also served as models, like letters about school business which the headteacher made available, and which were used as the children drafted their letters to adults connected with the refurbishment project. These prompted a modification in one of their letters, which had ended 'from', to 'yours sincerely', once they had checked what it meant. '*Yours sincerely* is just the same as *from*, but it's a better word, because it's more grown-up.' This comment again, although 'better' is perhaps ambiguous, places a perception about an individual word into the more macro context of what is appropriate for the text as a whole.

This use of models differs from that where children are sent to research a topic using library sources and to write something about it 'in their own words', which so often results in copying out extracts word for word. The reason for providing children with models as part of teaching them about language is less about the *content* of the text than about its *form*. Furthermore, children need to identify and transfer only those features of the text which are salient for the kind of text they are producing themselves.

'Texts', in this context, need not, of course, be written texts. Scenes from theatre or television drama may be the source of spoken texts to work with, as can radio broadcasts and sometimes spontaneous speech. In Chapter 2, I described a media studies project undertaken by a class of Year 5 children, in which they made a range of texts about their school, in different media. A member of the group which made a radio broadcast advertising the school to prospective parents wrote a summary of what they found out and were able to use in their own commercial from listening to a local commercial radio station, as well as from library research. The following extract from his report illustrates some of what he learned about a range of aspects of this kind of spoken text, from its generic features, such as the length, to micro concerns such as tone and pace of speech, to macro issues like the economics of airtime:

> We recorded some adverts from the radio because we wanted to find out how to make our radio advert and how long they should be. Most adverts are only 25 to 30 seconds long. We found out by listening that the people who are in the commercial speak in a lively voice to encourage the people who are listening to buy the things advertised. The person who is advertising speaks very fast because the people want to save money and time, because if they make it too long people

get bored. The adverts are expensive to make and you can't always be put on the radio station.

Data, evidence and investigation

Professional linguists make use of a combination of their own intuitive knowledge about language and data from the actual language produced by those who speak and write it as part of their daily experience. If you want to teach children about language, then it is important to help them to explore it, as the previous section on models suggested. The emphasis there was on the use of texts produced by others in the production of children's own written or spoken texts, but there are other ways in which evidence about language may be collected and investigated. The Cox Report advocated investigative approaches and the principle is a useful one to bear in mind: 'Work on knowledge about language can be based on pupils' own fieldwork, collecting and classifying their own data, learning about the methodology of observation, classification, description, hypothesis making and explanation' (DES, 1989: 6.12).

Written texts constitute one kind of 'evidence', and comparisons of different kinds of texts help to bring all kinds of features of language to the attention of those who investigate them, at whatever level they study them. When a primary school class embarks on a new topic, it is common for the teacher to collect a wide range of books to support the teaching; where funding allows, this is often supported by libraries. There is no need to stop at books, however. For a linguistic dimension to the topic, it is possible to make available in the classroom texts of other kinds, as well as books. The children can compare the texts across various dimensions, considering the form of each text, what they can find out about its intended audience, the style of presentation of its content, both in form – layout, typeface, headings and so on – and in relation to specific words and expressions used. When the texts under consideration differ from each other in genre, point of view, lexical choices and so on, then children's awareness of the operation of language is much more likely to be stimulated. McCarthy and Carter (1994) refer to this as the 'contrastive principle'.

An example of this was used with the Year 5 class who were involved in the media project described above. In order to explore the range of ways in which language is used in texts to perform different communicative jobs, the children were given a wide range of texts whose content was all connected to the same topic but for different purposes (T). The topic chosen was 'Trains', and the texts included story books for young children, historical accounts aimed at railway enthusiasts, timetables, publicity leaflets for season tickets with British Rail and for a local steam railway, postcards and so on. The children were asked to classify the texts in ways which made sense to them, and the activity caused lively discussion in the groups. Some children stuck to similarity of content as their deciding feature for each category, but others paid more attention to form. For example, one group divided the texts into five groups, under the headings: Leaflets, Tickets, Advertisements, Fiction and Non-Fiction. Another group used these categories: Books (subdivided into fiction and non-fiction), Not Books and Newspaper.

This example is from inside the classroom, but it is also possible, of course, to go outside and look at the language to be found around the school and in the wider environment. This may be tackled head on if the main purpose of the teaching is language itself, or more indirectly if the focus of the teaching is another topic but you are seeking to include a language dimension. Children can investigate the writing used in the school, considering its purpose, audience and form. In the light of some of the ideas explored in Chapter 5, they can find out, at their own level, more about all the ways in which written language keeps the school functioning, and about the complex lines of communication between different authors and their various audiences. Or, moving beyond the school gates, they can explore all the instances of writing to be found within a certain area, and, again, investigate how it got there, who wrote it and why, how it differs in function and form, and so on. If, however, the topic the children are studying is, for example, shopping, then texts associated with shopping will be read for their content but may also be investigated for their linguistic properties. The names of products and shops have their own histories and social connotations. The different kinds of information on product labels are not given equal prominence – another example of the connections between form and function. Curriculum topics with a historical dimension obviously create opportunities for comparison of language use in different times (LC). Likewise, geographical topics invite attention to languages used in different places (LV). Specialized vocabulary associated with specific areas of knowledge are often introduced by primary school teachers as a matter of course, but there is always scope to pay focused attention to new words from a linguistic point of view (LX).

The linguistic data available to children for investigation is not limited to written texts but includes the spoken language encountered every day. Children respond to different tones of voice, but they can be helped to articulate how they know how to 'read' differences in the way people speak to them. Varieties of languages people use, including local accents and dialects, can be the focus of study, and, again, it is obviously preferable to make use of collected data than to rely on prejudice and unsupported assumptions. Tape-recordings from the media, local informants or 'tape pals' in other parts of the country may provide such data, but it is important to remember that the descriptive, non-judgemental approach of the professional linguist cannot be taken for granted in children, especially if politicians and journalists cannot be relied on to set a good example! Adults and children may report that they cannot understand an unfamiliar accent or dialect, and this may have something to do with different people's processing of speech. However, even basic comprehensibility may be linked to attitude, and descriptions of the way others talk are often emotive, so a classroom ethos which discourages the denigration of other people on arbitrary grounds is important in tackling a topic like this.

On the other hand, such investigations do provide the opportunity to expose and explore myths and stereotypes and where they have come from. If children do have evaluative reactions to different accents, they can explore these, and the wider social forces which give rise to them (see Chapters 2 and 4).

Classifying data, looking for patterns

The process of learning anything is complex, but one of its facets is the apprehension of patterns which transform random phenomena into something comprehensible and capable of being retained in the memory. Linguists who are currently studying language in quite theoretical ways are interested in identifying the 'deep' structures which are characteristic of all human languages. Young children who are learning to speak are also, at their own level, 'seekers after meaning who try to find the underlying principles that will account for the patterns that they recognize in their experiences' (Wells, 1987: 43). Looking for patterns in linguistic data is an important aspect of developing knowledge about language, whether one is a theoretical linguist, an infant learning to talk, or a primary school child developing increasing competence in literacy and oracy.

The example of getting children to classify texts of different kinds, as described above and in Chapter 3, is one way of encouraging them to see beyond the content of different kinds of written language and focus on the fact that it takes many different forms, which are used to different effect in different contexts and by different audiences. Other things which are true about language also follow patterns which the children can look for. Being able to move from the specific to the general, in one direction, and from a generalized hypothesis or rule to its application in a particular instance, in the other, is another example of a way of approaching learning which will serve children well in many different subject areas, and even in relation to knowledge which they will need in future but which has yet to be discovered. Language, so ubiquitous throughout all human interaction, is awesome in its diversity, it is true, but systems and conventions are vital for it to be capable of conveying meaning among members of a given language-using community. By identifying for themselves what some of the rules and conventions of language are, children will not only find out more about language but also more about learning.

Within written texts there are of course many conventions which help the reader and upon which both reader and writer rely. Children can explore how texts of different kinds make use of paragraphing and other devices related to layout. They can be encouraged to suggest 'rules' which would account for the patterns they notice and set activities for their classmates to test these rules in other texts and in their own writing. This kind of approach may be applied to many aspects of written language, including punctuation and spelling. The English National Curriculum requires children to learn about patterns in common letter strings, for example, and the option is there for children to look for these themselves rather than being told by the teacher what they are in order merely to commit them to memory. Similarly, children can be equipped with reliable texts, such as well written story books, which contain instances of the need to distinguish dialogue from other sections of the text. How has the author indicated that one of the characters is speaking? From several examples, is it possible to derive a rule for the punctuation of speech? How does such a rule help the child who has discovered it to punctuate speech in her or his own writing? Can other children read this child's dialogue in context as its author intended?

In relation to spoken language, it is possible to describe the conventions which govern the ways in which people speak to each other differently according to the nature of their relationship and the context in which they are communicating, and children can find out more about this aspect of talk, using their own experience to generate hypotheses which can then be tested in interviews or by recording the dialogues of willing participants. Again, the 'interface' between the different modes of speech and writing provides a site for making aspects of language explicit. Punctuation has been described as the prosody of written language (Crystal, 1988: 212). In other words, there has to be some means of conveying to readers all the information which is carried by meaningful variations in the pitch, loudness, tempo and rhythm in spoken language. Examples include the rising intonation which, in English, characterizes a question, and the means by which speakers indicate the emphasis which, in writing, would warrant an exclamation mark. A 7-year-old child showed that she was interested in one of the differences between speech and writing when she asked her teacher how to surprise readers of her story. 'I know how you make someone jump when you're talking to them', she explained, 'but how do you do that in writing?' This kind of question, and the other conventions which help to make writing readable and unambiguous, may be investigated by children. They can use the texts around them to observe, record and make hypotheses about 'rules' which they can codify in their own terms.

Given that the accurate description of language is still occupying eminent linguists, and that it gives rise to conflict as well as consensus, it is probable that the children will meet problems. For example, it is unfortunate for teaching, though hardly surprising, that the words which break spelling 'rules' are often the most common. Many popular texts to be found in the 'real world', beyond what is written specially for children, flout conventions and, like advertising slogans, introduce both 'wrong' spellings and linguistic ambiguities. This need not, however, be a reason for sanitizing and idealizing the language which the children work with. The key is to find a balance between discovery and supportive input, an issue which is dealt with further below. However, it is always possible that in attempting to work out how to solve the problems to which written forms of language give rise, the children will discover useful rules for themselves, and they may even surprise the teacher with the ingenuity of their suggestions.

Authenticity and purpose

While language may well be an intrinsically interesting component of the world around us, and something which children do find fascinating, it is consistent with the principles of sound curriculum planning to contextualize linguistic investigations and, as far as possible, to provide children with tasks which have a meaning they can appreciate. It has already been suggested that work on language can be integrated into curriculum topics in various ways, using topics with a history, geography or science focus to look at a range of texts, at the discourses of different aspects of experience, at specialized vocabulary, and so on.

Work on language which is linked with the production of particular kinds of texts by the children provides opportunities for exploring how writers deal with specific aspects of language. Teachers frequently use situations where the children write sets of instructions in an authentic context to teach simultaneously about the process described and about the nature of instructional language. One example of this is the writing of recipes as part of a cookery lesson. Clarkson and Stansfield (1992) describe the learning about language which took place with a class of Year 3 children when a project on Italy involved making pizzas and writing about the process. The work included studying published recipes as models (T), which led to the redrafting of 'What to do' as 'Method', and, in the light of testing the original recipe exactly as it was written, to other amendments: 'We should have said to put the oven on first. We had to wait for it to get hot' (ibid.: 112).

Children are likely to learn about how language has to be manipulated to meet the needs of readers or listeners if they have opportunities to make their own texts with an authentic audience in mind. If they are aware that their writing is likely to be read only by their teacher, who clearly knows already as much about the topic as they do, and probably a great deal more, the incentive to make meaning explicit, unambiguous and appropriate for a specific genre is not there. It is well established that writing makes a number of simultaneous demands, particularly on children who are still learning the process. They have to think of the compositional aspects of writing, generating ideas and content, the communicative aspects, empathizing with the intended readers, and the secretarial aspects, controlling handwriting or keyboard, spelling and punctuation. It is difficult at any given time to give equal attention to all these dimensions, but authenticity of audience and purpose helps to make the communicative aspects less of a hypothetical abstraction, which may free the children to concentrate their thinking and produce more effective texts. The potential for promoting awareness of language through working on a specific text may be further exploited by setting children tasks which involve writing under some particular constraint, provided that authenticity and purpose are not sacrificed. Constraints could include a strict limit on the number of words in which a story is to be told, or having to conform to a recognized poetic form, such as a set number of lines and a pre-planned rhyming scheme.

In addition to the examples I have already given of children adapting their writing to meet more precisely the demands of its genre and intended audience, the following, from Cherrington (1987), is another instance of the importance of authenticity in providing an opportunity for children to refine their writing to meet the needs of its audience. It also illustrates how these children tackled the difference between spoken language, with its potential for an ironic intonation, and a written text in which the irony could well be lost. A group of 8- and 9-year-old girls decided to write an informative and persuasive book about cruelty to animals in captivity in zoos and circuses, for which they undertook research from books, from leaflets produced by the RSPCA and from a visit to a zoo, where they interviewed an education officer. The intended audience for their book was other children, mainly of their own age, but they wanted it to be accessible to as many children as possible. For one part of the book, two of the girls decided to present some of the information from one of the leaflets:

Donna: On the arrival of the small elephants they have to, um.
Ann: They won't understand what 'on arrival' means.
Donna: Of course they will.
Ann: Small children in the first year might not know.
Donna: They will.

At this point they turned to their teacher for arbitration. It is interesting that this phrase was identified as potentially difficult for younger readers, as it is an example of the grammatical construction known as 'nominalization', where an event which might have been described as a full clause with a verb, as in *when the small elephants arrive*, is converted into a noun phrase – *On the arrival of the small elephants* (G). These are sometimes cited as the kind of constructions, typical of non-fiction texts, which cause problems for young readers (see, for example, Perera, 1984). It is certainly true, and this may have influenced Anna, that children rarely use this kind of construction in their own writing. However, as Donna believed, the fact that children would be unlikely to *write* this does not necessarily mean that they could not understand it if they *read* it. Again, it is at the interface between reading and writing that aspects of language come to children's attention, and empathizing with readers is possible only when they contemplate an authentic audience.

In the second extract, the children faced the even more perplexing challenge of how writers can persuade readers to cooperate in the intended reading of a text. Susan and Ann were composing the introduction to the book. They had decided to address their readers directly, to confront them with the horror of seeing animals exploited for entertainment. Ann read aloud what they had written so far, using a very sarcastic tone of voice, which, if heard, would encourage the listener to answer 'of course not!'

Ann: How would you like a circus ticket, see the lions jumping through fire hoops, see the acrobats doing jumps off the dolphins?
Susan: I don't think they'll read it like that though will they?

Ann: Mmm.
Susan: They'll sort of read it like this – [reading with no particular expression]
'How would you like a . . . circus ticket', they'll just read it won't they?

The children solved the problem by adding a new sentence at the bottom of this first page, which read 'Now turn over and see if you still want the circus ticket!'

Of course it is impractical to arrange for every piece of writing to have an actual audience outside the classroom, and for every text produced to be complete and on a subject about which the children feel as committed as this group did so that their encounters with problems about spoken, written and read language had the potential for teaching them many things about language itself. Neither should it be forgotten that one 'authentic' purpose for producing and responding to language in school is the process of teaching and learning. School lessons cannot – and should not – become one extended simulation. However, it is possible to bear in mind the usefulness of authenticity and to maximize the opportunities to plan for it. A compromise which may be available between authentic contexts for work with language (which may, of course, be spoken as well as written, as in drama and role play, for example) is to simulate audiences, specifying for the children quite explicitly who they should *imagine* is going to read their work. An example of this is when children choose characters from fairy stories as writers and recipients of letters, a device used to effect in the book of letters *The Jolly Postman* (Ahlberg and Ahlberg, 1986) and often followed up by teachers. The role play and writing which are often incorporated into geography and history are another obvious context for learning about language. While imaginary or simulated contexts for using language may lack actual authenticity, they provide a wider range than is possible otherwise, and are surely an improvement on arid exercises undertaken from textbooks.

The role of the teacher

The foregoing sections emphasize the appropriateness of recognizing children's existing knowledge about language and using investigative approaches which encourage them to collect their own data and find out patterns for themselves. However, being a teacher is not only about being a facilitator. The section of the Cox Report quoted above (under 'Data, evidence and investigation') which advocates investigative approaches continues: 'The teacher's task will often be to help pupils to systematize knowledge which they already have or evidence which they collect, and to keep the focus clear' (DES, 1989: 6.12). The demands currently placed on primary school teachers are manifold: handling all the areas of the curriculum, providing sophisticated pastoral support, managing assessment issues and keeping detailed records available for inspection, along with a range of plans and policies. The ideal of simultaneously being alert for every opportunity to raise individual children's consciousness of language at precisely the optimum moment, and to have every project skilfully devised to incorporate the most relevant aspect of linguistic pattern finding, is no doubt unrealistic. However, as I suggested at the start of this chapter, it is not impossible to bear in mind the general principles and to plan for teaching about language in the context of most project, topic and literacy work. In the next chapter we shall consider a range of examples of ways in which teachers have successfully undertaken such teaching about language, but I conclude here with a checklist of things to consider in curriculum planning so as to maximize opportunities for children to learn about language itself.

Variety in reading

All the points above have emphasized the variety of experience with language which is essential if children are to develop their awareness and understanding of language. In planning a sequence of teaching, consider the range of texts which could be incorporated into what you are planning to do. This does not necessarily mean that you should always cast around for extensive variety, but rather that, over a period such as a term, there should be opportunities for the children to engage with texts in a variety of media, with different functions and different intended audiences.

Variety in writing

Again, it is helpful to keep a checklist of the range of audiences for whom children have written during a given period and to ensure that there has been sufficient range for the knowledge about language which is born of experiences with writing to be fostered. Have the children written for an audience not known to them? Have they had opportunities to write in formal and informal styles? Have they written instructions and opinions as well as stories?

Variety in spoken language

Awareness of different registers and of the range of speaking styles appropriate for different audiences develops through experience. Have the children had opportunities to talk to different people for different purposes and to role play an even wider range of verbal experience? What is there in the current teaching topic which lends itself to the exploration of different kinds of talking? Encounters with a character from history? A lecture by a pupil-as-scientist explaining to an unenlightened audience some aspect of the physical world and its properties?

Drawing out knowledge about language

The mere opportunity to use language in all these different ways will not in itself ensure that the children learn about it at a conscious level. It is the teacher's job to anticipate features of language which might arise and to ensure that they are developed. For example, does a planned drama session create opportunities for some explicit work on the differences between standard and non-standard English? Between the children's perusal of some relevant texts and their drafting of their own, there may need to be a lesson in which features of the kinds of text under review are drawn out and made explicit. There will be a need to balance the macro and the micro aspects of language. In other words, while some considerations will be at a whole-text level, and will arise from the realities of language as a social practice, these have implications for much finer detail, like legibility of handwriting, accuracy of spelling, or perhaps the origins of words with a common spelling pattern, which may be lifted from the context of the whole project and focused on in detail. Which children are ready to benefit from some detailed teaching about particular aspects of punctuation? Does the topic include some unfamiliar vocabulary and where, if at all, does this fit into the children's investigations of spelling patterns?

Opportunities for reflection

There will need to be direct input from the teacher on aspects of language, so that the children not only make explicit their existing knowledge but also learn new information and new ways of making sense of what they know. There is also scope for the children themselves to consider what they have learnt and to put it into words. Is there room at points during the topic to have the children reflect on data they have collected, patterns they have identified, new knowledge they have gained? This can be built into text production, for example by writing an account for another group of things they need to know in order to write a book for infants, put together a radio broadcast, devise a word puzzle on the computer and so on.

Another important dimension of reflective learning is learning to be aware of oneself as a learner. Information and advice for teachers about the different strategies which work for different children often omit to point out that children can help themselves – and you – by raising to consciousness various things which they find helpful in their own learning. While some children seem to learn to spell easily, for example, for others it presents problems which they need help to overcome. This fact itself can provide the basis for some teaching about language, if teachers address directly the fact that spelling is a challenge and work cooperatively with the children on strategies which help learners with different styles. Children can investigate how different people they know tackle spellings, using and displaying in the classroom visual links, mnemonics and rhymes to record useful suggestions. Research suggests that the link between the hand and the eye is important for establishing spellings in long-term memory (see, for example, Peters, 1985), so for many children tactile experiences like tracing words with the finger or guessing what a partner is 'writing' on their back or hand can be helpful. Learning about how they visualize spellings by reflecting on the process and trying to 'read' a word of which only the top or bottom half is visible will focus their attention, and they need to know that the strategy of 'Look – Cover – Write – Check' must involve visualizing the word after looking at it for long enough to commit it to memory. It is not only spelling which can be the focus of children's reflections on their own learning, but many other aspects of the language curriculum too. Finding out whether they tackle reading, writing and tasks involving talk in the same way as their friends can be informative for children and also for their teachers.

Conclusion

This chapter has outlined some possibilities for teaching about language in the context of everyday classroom practice. I have suggested that teaching about language is best thought of as an integral part of the curriculum and not necessarily under the headings of talking, reading or writing, but in the interface between them. I have advocated having in mind a clear rationale for planning teaching about language, and suggested that you need to look out for incidental opportunities for raising awareness of language as a medium of communication to children's conscious attention, as well as planning tasks which are designed to promote this consciousness raising. The idea that genuine collaboration between children, as opposed to unfocused work in groups, is likely to make children more explicit about language choices has been explored, as has the potential of a wide range of authentic texts encountered in reading as examples of what other, more experienced writers have produced. The principle of seeing texts as data which can be investigated in the pursuit of knowledge about language has been put forward, and one of the methods for doing this is to classify data, identifying and making use of patterns. Language work which has an authentic purpose is more likely to be successful in developing children's knowledge about and understanding of language, but where variety in purpose and audience is not possible, teachers can plan for simulated contexts for the texts under production.

Earlier chapters have observed that teaching about language may need to be a combination of facilitating investigations and providing explicit information and instruction, and the final section of this chapter has suggested that the teacher has an important role in providing supportive contexts for children to learn about language. These include access to a wide variety of texts, both written and spoken, and opportunities to think about and learn about language as it is used in schools and in the wider community. The next chapter will present further examples of children learning about language in the primary school, and we shall also consider the question of assessment, in the light of the requirements of the 1995 English National Curriculum.

7 Teaching about language: topics, projects and plans

Introduction

The previous chapter outlined some principles to serve as a guide for plans concerned with teaching children about language. This chapter presents a range of activities which provide opportunities for children to learn more about language. These are grouped loosely under a number of themes and include suggestions for work which could be incorporated into various components of the curriculum, as well as describing in greater detail some projects which would offer opportunities for more extended schemes of work. The final section considers the issues of planning schemes of work and assessing children's achievements.

It will be evident from what was said in Chapter 3 about progression that the kinds of activities which you can plan in order to increase your pupils' knowledge about language will be adaptable for different age groups, and will not need to follow a rigid chronological sequence. Chapter 6 also suggested that learning about language is not mode specific, that the 'interface' of reading and writing provides particular opportunities for language awareness, and that knowledge about language develops as children reflect on their experiences of talk, reading and writing, usually by talking about them, but also by writing about what they have learned and sometimes by reading the reflections of others (for a diagrammatic representation of this see Richmond, 1990: 41). This chapter does not, therefore, present teaching suggestions under the headings of the National Curriculum attainment targets, since the activities suggested usually involve at least two of the three targets and often all of them.

In fact, there will always be overlaps between any grouping of topics for language study, and the sections into which I have divided the suggestions are to some extent arbitrary. For example, the multilingual dictionary project which is described under 'Focusing on words' could equally well have appeared under 'Making texts about language' or 'Exploring language varieties'. What I have tried to do is to include a range of starting points and ways of thinking about language-based work which are adaptable to different teaching priorities and ways of working. Once again, I have referred to Figure 2.1, which illustrates the macro and micro levels of topics within teaching about language, to indicate the kinds of areas covered in each teaching suggestion (see page 28). It is possible to ensure that any teaching activity which starts with texts and data at the core will cover aspects of the bottom line of Figure 2.1, the micro aspects, the elements of English (and other languages) described in Chapter 1, but that the macro issues and larger topics outlined on the top line will also be addressed.

Making texts about language

The production of texts *about* language has obvious potential for encouraging children to reflect on language itself. As pupils, they are familiar with texts about literacy, from the colourful materials encountered in the infant reading classroom to the English textbooks which are likely to be among the stock of many primary schools, and are for sale to anxious parents in their local bookshops.

Richmond (1990) describes children in a Year 1 class who made a number of alphabet friezes relating to three of the languages spoken in the class (LV). Work on the alphabet, of course, is a basis for the phonic work associated with literacy (P/O), and could be extended so that the children produce other texts to help with their own and other children's learning about the phonic aspects of reading (LA). Many of the wall charts which teachers display in the classroom to remind children about topics such as letter combinations could be supplemented by children themselves doing the investigative and productive work involved in making their own posters.

In Sealey (1992) I described a project in which some Year 6 children devised dictionaries of their own 'street language', making entries for those words 'which you and your friends know and use but which you think adults would not use' (p. 55). This project involved the children taking a fresh look at dictionaries. They had to think about the purpose of dictionaries. Are they for looking up correct spellings (P/O) (and who decided what is 'correct'?) or for looking up definitions (S) (and who decides what these are? (LS)). They considered more carefully the notion of audience, from children's 'first dictionaries' to those for learners of a foreign language, to very detailed adult dictionaries, and so on. And their attention was drawn to the genre of a reference book like this, and to its discourse style (T). As one of the children said, in order to make their dictionary look authentic they had to learn 'parts of speech, like the little *n*.s and *adj*.s . . . and the way things are set out'. So classifying words into different groups was part of the learning about language (LX, S), as was discussion about how words have changed over time (LC), the significance of offensive words (LS) and the precise meanings of the words they had selected (S). The data which drove this project, then, were linguistic data from their own experience. The texts were the models provided by published dictionaries (reading) and the dictionaries they produced themselves (writing).

The Year 5 children who made the radio broadcast which is referred to in various places in this book finished their work on the project by making a further tape of guidelines for children who might do a similar media project in future years. They adapted the style to appeal to child listeners, reporting what they had learned about this medium and its texts.

Other texts about language include word puzzles, which the children can set for each other. Devising crosswords, riddles and even word-search puzzles requires children to draw on what they know about words and their meanings (S) and about spelling (P/O). There is a strong motivation for checking their spellings since their puzzles will fail if they have been inaccurately set. Such activities, again, can be adapted for the age and experience of the children, and a substantial project aimed at producing language-puzzle books, or a Christmas annual, for instance, for a specified audience (such as children in another class or school) could be developed if appropriate for your teaching plans, but this would not be essential.

Focusing on words

Dictionaries as texts for children to work on provide one context for focusing on language at the level of words (LX, S). They can also offer a particular perspective on language variety (LV) if the textual product is an interlanguage dictionary. This again is something which can be tackled, particularly in multilingual classes, with various age groups. The degree of sophistication would, of course, increase as the children had greater knowledge to draw on, and younger children might produce a wall chart or poster rather than a full-length dictionary, with the words for topical curriculum items in a number of languages. More experienced children can become involved in the notation of the pronunciation of words which might be unfamiliar to non-native speakers, which is what happened when one teacher worked with some Year 7 children on thematic dictionaries in English, Panjabi and Urdu, about fruit and animals. Their challenge was to represent not only the words in the appropriate scripts but to include also a phonetic guide to pronunciation (P/O). Similar work could be done in relation to dialect words, from the locality or using television programmes as the source of data.

Written words, of course, are often the focus of children's attention in the context of spelling (P/O). In addition to these practical aspects, there is also the factual information about words and their origins which offers support for spelling (LC). Breaking words down into – or building them up from – their morphological parts reminds children of the patterns which characterize many English words (P/O), as well as drawing attention to the 'foreign imports' (LV) which are subject to different rules. Again, the children themselves can be the authors of texts for the classroom wall or library which share and preserve the knowledge about words which they have acquired.

As was pointed out in the discussion above about the limitations of teaching about the elements of language in isolation, single words are relatively infrequent in texts we encounter every day, but this is something which could be explored as an interesting proposition with children. In their data collection for language work, they can be encouraged to look out for one-word texts and discover what, if anything, they have in common. One property of such texts is that the brevity needed for impact (as on the crossing patrol's *STOP*) relies on the legitimate expectation that the reader will supply much of the missing meaning from the context, and children can be encouraged to make explicit what these implied meanings are (LS). (What mistakes might a Martian visitor make if this cultural information was not clear? For example, is it compulsory to obey the imperative *PUSH* written on the shop door? What about a nearby sign which says *LIFT*? What is the difference? Is there the basis for a story here?)

Another kind of text which uses individual words – or very short phrases – is that which indicates the name of some part of the environment, such as a street, a shop or a house. The non-statutory guidance which accompanied the original English National Curriculum suggested 'Names and Terms' as a project to promote the understanding of language for pupils at Key Stages 1 and 2. Bartlett and Fogg (1992) developed these ideas, and one group in the Year 6 class they worked with investigated the origins of local street names (LS, LC). Another group looked at shop names, classifying them into categories, which included owners' names, names to do with what was being sold, and 'funny' names, a category which they subdivided according to their language properties: rhyme, alliteration (P/O) and metaphor (S). Another group wrote to the residents of local houses which had names, receiving letters of explanation so that another type of text was incorporated into the work. This project extended to include an exploration of the origins of personal names, and so more reference books (another type of authentic text) were drawn on in this teaching about language.

Children can experiment with the connotations and associations of words to see whether single words have identical meanings for everyone (S). The archetypal word association game, where one person says a word and a partner says the first word which comes to mind, is one way of revealing this, and it can be adapted as a group game with participants issuing challenges and supplying justifications. Individual words with rich cultural and metaphorical associations can form the basis of a short exploration, beginning with a brainstorm to reveal how familiar the children are with these, and extending to investigate the phrases in which the word features. Keith (unpublished paper) suggests the word 'green' as a good candidate for a piece of work like this. In English, three powerful sets of associations with 'green' are envy, youth and environmental concerns, but the children may also be able to supply figurative connotations from other cultural influences.

Children can investigate how much meaning an individual word can carry, and how much depends on other clues. One activity which explores this is to write individual words on pieces of card. The children, working in pairs, place their word in the centre of a large piece of paper and draw and write around it as many clues and associations as they can think of to make it possible for another pair to guess their word once it has been removed from the paper. If you include some functional or grammatical words with the content or lexical words (see Chapter 1), this is a good way to introduce the concept of these two categories (G), as children will find it difficult to draw and write clues for functional words. This can be extended by getting the children to add to the lists and testing whether they were right by letting another pair provide clues. Some work of this kind was used as preparation for the dictionary project described above, to explore knowledge of single words and the nature of dictionary definitions.

Riddles focus on individual words, drawing sometimes on spelling (P/O), sometimes on connotations of words and sometimes on double meanings (S). Spelling riddles involve clues of the genre:

> My first is in book but never in boat
> My second's in nail but never in float. . . .

The kind of riddle included in *The Hobbit* and many other children's stories draws more on unusual or misleading descriptions of the familiar, such as:

> A box without hinges, key or lid,
> Yet golden treasure inside is hid.

Tolkien, 1966: 70

Both kinds may also make use of rhyme and rhythm and the details of language systems, but, as *The Hobbit* illustrates, there is a social element to them too (LS). As Bilbo engages in the riddle game with Gollum, he reflects 'that the riddle game was sacred and of immense antiquity, and even wicked creatures were afraid to cheat when they played it' (ibid.: 74). Children can solve riddles, work out together how they have been constructed and make up their own. These activities, again, could be developed to form part of a collection of puzzle books for other children.

The structures of texts

Teaching about language which assumes whole texts as the unit of study puts the investigation of words and sentences into context. This contrasts with the traditional emphasis where reading stories or information books is a completely separate activity from the lesson in grammar. By making use in the language curriculum of the texts which the children are reading for pleasure or to support their project work you will not only use time more efficiently, but connections between these different aspects of language in use should also be more apparent to the children.

Written texts have an internal structure which is more than just a sequence of sentences (G). One way of drawing children's attention to this is by *dis*-connecting the text and letting them put it back together. You can decide on where to make the breaks depending on the children's experience and abilities, cutting up a copy of a short text into smaller or larger 'chunks' such as sentences or paragraphs.

With narratives, children are likely to find it relatively easy to assemble beginnings and endings in the right place, especially if there are formulaic clues like *Once upon a time* and *They all lived happily ever after*. Narratives are also likely to include other signals in the text which indicate the chronology – phrases like *after that, as soon as, then*. Or one phrase may be used to refer to a whole idea, like *this cunning plan*. Children may not know at first what clues they are using, but, especially if they collaborate, they will become increasingly expert at making use of references forward and back in the text, thus developing the important concept of cohesion. They may be aware below the level of consciousness that the first reference to a character is likely to use the indefinite article – once there was *a* fierce lion – but that subsequent references will be to *the* lion. Dialogue is usually structured so that the speakers' turns are obvious, and this can help with sequencing the whole text. The teacher's role here may be to prompt with questions such as, 'How did you know? Which words gave you clues?', so that, again, features of the text's cohesive properties are raised to the children's conscious attention.

In non-narrative texts, the children will have to use some different clues to resequence a disassembled text successfully (see Chapter 5). There may be phrases such as *on the other hand*, or *however*, which demonstrate an 'adversative' relationship between one part of the text and another. There may also be references to causal relationships, through words such as *therefore* and *as a result of this*. Practice in finding the part of the text to which such a *this* refers, by handling the pieces of text and trying out different sequences, helps children to learn more about text structure and can carry over into their own writing, particularly if you make explicit reference to the knowledge they have gained.

The possibilities available in the physical management of texts are extended enormously by the resources of information technology. Children who have learned various word-processing skills can explore the structure of texts by experimenting on the screen without the restrictions of limited copies or the need to rewrite. However, you may need to spend some preparation time exploring the limits and potential of the particular hardware and software which are available, as well as giving thought to the distribution of these resources among an entire class.

A variation on this approach to teaching about the structure of texts is to supply various parts of a target text but have the children complete it. It is a familiar strategy for teachers to give children the opening few sentences of a story to be completed from their own creative resources, but this is usually seen as a stimulus to the imagination rather than as a language teaching point. Support for the apprentice report writer as well as for the budding author of fiction can be offered in the form of a 'signposted' text, only part of which has to be created by the individual child. Of course it is important not to imply that there is one definitive way of writing a report on a technology project, say, or a field visit, but making the building blocks available for children to incorporate into their own texts may be more helpful than merely exhorting them to 'write in complete sentences' as a means of producing an appropriate report.

Various approaches have been developed to help children with the structure of narratives, adapting the analyses evolved in literary research to help young children. The main stages of the classic narrative genre (as outlined in Labov, 1972) are: the abstract, which indicates what the story will be about; the orientation, which introduces the participants, the location and the circumstances of the action; the complicating action, which is its events or problems; the evaluation or point of the story; and the resolution, which brings the story to a recognizable end. Using a story planner, which divides these elements into parts of a story which children can recognize, can help children to make their own stories more sophisticated and successful. One teacher of a Year 2 class (Mason, 1991) discussed familiar stories with her pupils using the following headings: Type of story; Time; Setting; Characters' names; Description of characters; Ideas for the plot; Ending. She went on to encourage the children to plan their own stories under the same headings and was gratified with the improvements on the lengthy but sometimes unwieldy stories they had been producing before. Similar approaches can become a routine aid for children at Key Stage 2, who can learn to adapt the basic structure and extend their competence as story writers.

Spoken narratives have been shown to follow similar structures, while other kinds of spoken exchange, such as a shopping transaction, include recognizable elements. (These are not necessarily the same in different cultures.) Children can investigate these through role plays, drama and transcripts. More sophistication may be needed to examine the combinations of spontaneous spoken language, scripted language, written captions and visual images found in different kinds of television programme.

Exploring language varieties

It was suggested in the previous chapter that a key aspect of teaching about language is raising children's consciousness, making the familiar strange and available for explicit attention. The experience of contrast helps to do this and the topic of language variety offers contrasts at various levels. Variety of genre and of discourse type have been used in several of the examples given above, and it has been suggested that children can experiment with another variable, such as the intended audience, to see what effect this has on the choices made in grammar and lexis. In other words, suppose a child lost her games kit on the way to school by getting involved in a prank with some other children. Versions of the narrative about that one event are likely to vary as the story is told to (1) her teacher, (2) her best friend, and (3) her mother. This kind of variation is a useful focus for many types of teaching about language and you may remember that 'variety' in the range of texts encountered in children's talk, reading and writing was a key principle discussed in the previous chapter.

However, the dimension of 'variety' in language which usually comes to mind is between and within languages in relation to speech communities, and many language awareness programmes start with the large-scale differences between one language and another (LV). A survey of the different languages spoken in the school or class is a worthwhile investigation for the children to undertake, and the results are often surprising in the range of languages covered, especially if the children find out from family members which languages they can speak. There are often problems to solve connected with the names given to different languages, and you may need to prepare some reference material for the children to use in their research. Another issue which is likely to be thrown up is how well someone has to know a language before it should be recorded in the survey (LA). Does knowing a few words count? If not, how much does someone need to know? Must the informant be literate in the language or is fluent speaking ability sufficient? In what circumstances do people speak the different languages they know (LS)? Is there a pattern? Compiling questions for a survey is a useful activity in itself, a chance to handle data about language and to be involved in the kind of text which requires the construction of interrogative rather than declarative sentences (G). It also offers an opportunity to interpret and classify responses.

Of course differences in language are often associated with social and cultural differences, and children who are fluent speakers of languages which may be seen as low status may deny their knowledge or feel embarrassed unless the ethos in the school is quite clearly positive towards linguistic and cultural diversity. If work of this kind is new it is usually helpful for teachers or confident visiting adults to be the first people to demonstrate knowledge of languages other than English, particularly if bilingual children are in a small minority.

Other texts which would be relevant for this kind of topic include translation dictionaries, and in many local education authorities support services have produced materials in and about the main languages used in the locality. Children can explore the similarities and differences between scripts across languages, and hypothesize about patterns, such as which symbols in an unfamiliar script might be punctuation, and whether the script has a sound–symbol correspondence or not (P/O). Something like punctuation may be more noticeable in a foreign language because of the distancing which the unfamiliar brings about, a resource for teaching about English punctuation.

Children can listen to story tapes read in a range of languages and compare the written versions in dual-language books, which are increasingly available from mainstream publishers and should be a resource in any classroom where language is the subject of study, not only in schools attended by bilingual children.

The study of variety within language allows for work on accent and dialect, and takes the concept of linguistic diversity to a slightly more detailed level. After all, the contrast between completely different scripts, alphabets, lexis and grammar is impossible to ignore, but people are remarkably inaccurate in their perceptions of their own regional accents, and regional expressions may not be recognized as such until they cause misunderstandings.

One way to generate texts for investigation here is through drama and role play. Rather than being asked to focus consciously on differences in regional varieties of talk, children may be more successful if they think themselves into the role of people who use language in particular ways, undertaking the analysis afterwards. They may well have stereotyped ideas, so it is useful to have available tapes and videos for comparison. Many children will describe received pronunciation as 'posh' and attach other social meanings to various accents (LS). You can encourage greater precision by getting the children to listen closely to the way English is pronounced in different accents and they can experiment with phonetic representations (P/O). This may also be the place to introduce more accurate terminology.

Many texts which make use of regional accents and dialects are published in the form of books available from, for example, tourist shops and heritage centres, and there are many dialect versions of narratives like Bible stories and traditional folk tales in books and sometimes on tape. Some novels include dialogue in regional accents or with dialect features. Again, children can investigate these from various points of view, including the degree of the writer's success in conveying accent (P/O), the dialect features found in the text, which older children could attempt to classify (LX, G), and the reasons for the different social attitudes towards different ways of speaking (LS).

It is in the context of a sequence of work like this that the vexed issue of standard English might be explicitly taught (LV, LS, P/O, LX, G). The overwhelming majority of the texts which children read are written predominantly in standard English, so that contrastive work on texts which make use of dialect features can illuminate the differences. Because of the social stigma associated with not 'talking properly', it may be more sensitive to begin an exploration of the nature and significance of non-standard features by using videos from television programmes, including those featuring English as it is spoken outside Britain (in Australia, for example), rather than homing in on the local variety straight away. If this heightens the children's awareness of what to look for (i.e. unfamiliar words and syntactical structures, the difference between accent and dialect, and so on), their growing expertise may then be deployed in any discussions of the non-standard features which children are required by our national legislation not to use in much of their written work. In any case, it is helpful to you to know how accurately your pupils can identify recurring non-standard features in their own writing, and, once these have been identified, they are in a position to consider for themselves what sorts of strategies they find useful in remembering the standard forms in those contexts where they want to be able to use them. You might also want to show older children some examples of texts in the complaint tradition (see

Chapter 4). If so, the opinion and letters columns of local newspapers are a good source.

Another axis across which language varies is time, with the differences between older and more contemporary texts forming a contrast which, again, brings language to children's conscious notice (LC, LV). One obvious context for integrating this kind of investigation into the curriculum is when the topic has a historical theme. Resources which support this kind of work can be found among history sources which reproduce old documents and in historical fiction where attempts are made to recreate the style of English spoken in different periods. Children can be encouraged to identify words whose meanings have changed or which are completely unfamiliar, and can research from dictionaries or reference books their meanings and origins (LX, S). They may also notice syntactical differences between modern and older versions of English, which is helpful in providing a context for focusing on grammar (G).

Change in language does not always have to be studied across long time spans, however. Sensitive as children are to fashion, they may be more aware than you are of the most contemporary slang and the need to avoid that which has become dated. This point was made by the children who made the *Dazzlers' Dictionary* described above. They reflected on the difference between some of their expressions and those used by their parents and teachers, and on the importance of being in the know about certain words, as one girl explained:

> . . . some people, who aren't – like – who don't get in with the gang and all the fashionable words, they just say normal words, but the other people that are with it all they say all fashionable words . . .

This discussion included two opinions about the fate of current slang. While most children expected it to sound old-fashioned by the time they were grown up, one boy wondered if it would become part of everyday, mainstream language.

Writing which is intended for children may include dialogue which dates it at a particular time, and children could research the children's language used in novels by CS Lewis, Enid Blyton and more recent authors, for example, although there they are likely to notice variety associated with class (LS) as well as period. Because written texts lag behind innovations in spoken language, radio and television can be a good source of data for looking at changes in spoken language. For example, Smith (1992) describes work with children in Years 5 and 6 which made use of two television programmes, an extract from an episode of *Watch with Mother* broadcast in 1963 and one from *Take Hart* in 1990. The children drew on their knowledge of media texts and conventions in their comparison, which also addressed body language, the language of instructions, changes in the use of words (the frequent use of *pretty* and *splendid* were two examples), voice quality and accent. The author notes that there was scope for the introduction of more precise metalanguage to help the children express their observations accurately, and that the topic provided a potential context in which to explore standard English.

Focusing on grammar

The pitfalls in treating sentence-level grammar out of context have been stressed, but the knowledge that groups of words function in accordance with syntactical rules (G) is helpful to children, and may be approached from the starting point of texts rather than abstractions.

One text which has been used as a model for looking at sentence structure is the *Mix or Match Storybook* (Scarry, 1980). Each page of this picture book, which is aimed at young children, is divided into six sections, with a spiral binder which allows the pages to be flipped over in sections, to make 'more than 200,000 comical combinations', as the front cover proclaims. Each section has a colourful picture with a caption consisting of part of a sentence, and all the sentences follow the same structural pattern. Thus the first page (or sentence) reads: 'Lowly Worm / was driving an apple car / through Busytown / when Postman Pig tripped / and delivered the mail / into Mrs Pig's bubble bath.' The second page (or sentence) reads: 'Rudolf Von Strudel / was flying an aeroplane / over the airport / when Mr Paint Pig lost his balance / and spilled a can of red paint / into a musician's tuba.' These are complex sentences and a secondary school teacher who used them with her Year 8 children to produce their own picture books in the same format noted that the children found the structure quite challenging. However, the idea could be simplified to provide equivalent metalinguistic opportunities for younger children. One modification would be for the model sentences to be much simpler; another would be for the teacher to work with the children, making a big version of the book by taking suggestions and discussing them before committing them to a large piece of paper which everyone could see. Another approach would be for the teacher to prepare sections of various sentences on pieces of card which the children could sort out and put in order before working in groups to copy the captions on to the appropriate pieces of card with their illustrations. This kind of teacher involvement is advisable because it is unlikely that all the suggestions made by the children will 'work' syntactically, although if you do allow the children free rein to experiment with the elements of a complex sentence you will gain some insight into the categories they are using, and any 'errors' may be instructive.

Another variation on this theme is to let the children experiment with combining the elements of sentences which you have written out on to cards of different colours. Noun phrases might be green, for example, verb phrases blue and miscellaneous function words red. This would apply to the sentences from the fold-over book as follows.

Green: Lowly Worm, an apple car, Busytown, Postman Pig, the mail, Mrs Pig's bubble bath, Rudolf Von Strudel, an aeroplane, the airport, Mr Paint Pig, his balance, a can of red paint, a musician's tuba.

Blue: was driving, tripped, delivered, was flying, lost, spilled.

Red: through, when, and, into, over.

It is more useful to children to gain some insight into how noun phrases relate to verbs than to be able to identify precisely the word class to which each element belongs. Having experimented with various combinations, the children could try adding to the words in each category by writing new words and phrases on to the appropriate colour of card, and, once again, their 'errors' are likely to be instructive to you about their level of understanding.

An extension of this kind of activity is to move beyond declarative sentences, which is the category to which these examples belong, and experiment with imperatives, losing the inflectional ending on the head verbs – *Spill the paint!*, *Deliver the mail!* – and questions. To make interrogatives, the children would need to cut up the verb phrases to release *was* for the first position in their sentences, or to add new *wh-* words such as *who* or *when*.

An important final stage after an activity like this is to encourage the children to reflect on what they have learned. They could try to formulate 'rules' which explain how their combinations could make standard English sentences and what would not work. Some basic grammatical terminology is likely to prove essential during a sequence of work like this. Remember that, following the principles outlined in the previous chapter, there is always the potential to carry the experience of focusing directly on grammatical categories into other work, so that when the children ask about the spelling of a word in the course of their writing, for example, you can ask them to consider whether it would come into the 'green', 'blue' or 'red' group as used in this activity.

Some opportunities to highlight aspects of syntax will arise in the context of most kinds of writing activity, especially if the variables of purpose, audience and genre are providing the range required in the National Curriculum and advocated in the previous chapter. Harriott (1990) describes one of these incidental opportunities. A class of Year 3 children produced two types of record of their experience of baking bread, a class book of photographs with captions, and individual journals which recorded the process as a report. It was striking that the children had, quite appropriately, used predominantly past tense forms for their journal entries and present tense for the captions. The teacher took just a few minutes to draw attention to the contrast, encouraging the children to articulate the difference between the two kinds of sentence, and introduce the general categories of past and present tense, which have different uses and convey different meanings.

Careful transcription of short stretches of spontaneous spoken language may be contrasted with written equivalents, to raise awareness of the differences between the two modes. If children have to find a metalanguage to describe the different features, they will almost inevitably begin to discuss the syntax of the two kinds of text.

Playing with language

The suggestions given so far in this chapter for teaching children – or helping them to learn – about language have taken texts as their central focus, and have, I hope, demonstrated that learning about language can be interesting and relevant to children and teachers. We should not forget in addition that language has a 'ludic' (or playful) function: playing with language, as well as being enjoyable, can be a means of finding out more about its properties and its potential.

The children who made the *Dazzlers' Dictionary* talked about the function of slang as a means of excluding outsiders from certain discussions (LS), and children can have fun inventing various linguistic codes for doing this. The concept of language as a code is often presented by getting children to invent and crack coded messages, and this can be extended to explorations of back-slang and variations on it. Crystal (1987: 59) outlines a wide range of ways in which the forms of words are disrupted to make them unintelligible to out-siders, and children could experiment with these systems, such as messages which use only the first letters of words, or the first sounds (not necessarily the same thing – P/O).

Riddles have been mentioned above, although they are obviously relevant here too, as are many kinds of jokes and puns. The play on words which is involved in 'knock-knock' jokes, for example, relies on coincidences of phono-logical patterns (P/O) and ambiguities (S). For instance, the answer to 'Who's there?' may be 'Isabel', with the punch line 'Is a bell necessary on a bicycle?' Analysed linguistically, one proper noun, *Isabel*, is repeated as three separate words, *is a bell*, which are almost identical phonologically with the proper noun but which have different syntactical functions. There is an obvious danger in subjecting humour to this kind of analysis. The point of the joke is lost, and the analysis is likely to become burdensome to the children. Although know-ledge of well worn formulaic jokes often confers status with junior school children, they usually find it difficult to construct their own equivalent jokes successfully, despite being able to produce humorous contributions in other discursive contexts. Conversely, failing to 'get' a joke can be humiliating, all of which make the production of formula 'jokes' a limited context for teach-ing about language. Gibson (1992), making a similar point, places jokes in the classroom at the macro level (LS). He suggests that it is more appropriate to encourage children to reflect on the relationship between jokes and audiences, asking them to think for example about which jokes are suitable for friends but not teachers, and why; whether 'Irish' jokes are racist; whether girls and boys find the same kinds of joke funny, and so on. This approach, again, links micro and macro concerns about language and avoids the kind of analysis which destroys its own object.

However, the potential of crosswords, anagrams, palindromes, acrostics, rebuses, tongue twisters and so on for considering the patterns of language is not diminished if we accept that 'playing' with these may be different from dissecting language as 'humour'.

Rhymes, poems, advertisements

The final topic in this section links some particular genres which I think have potential to bring language to our conscious attention in several different ways.

Advertisements have a number of characteristics which lend themselves to teaching about language, some of which are shared with rhymes and poems, although from some points of view the forms are significantly different.

Advertisements are usually short texts, which need to deliver their message quickly to have an immediate impact. They make use of the connotations which cluster around particular words and images, exploiting cultural meanings and playing with the reader's or viewer's expectations. They are often densely intertextual, setting up mini-stories which remind the audience of other familiar texts: soap operas and grand operas, fairy tales, feature articles; and, increasingly, other advertisements. Even in their written form, they are often more dialogic than other written texts, addressing the reader directly, asking questions or posing problems from the point of view of the reader, problems to which the product, of course, offers a solution. Television commercials are technically slick and, since they are frequently repeated but also changed periodically, sometimes mimicking a serialized narrative, they can become part of the fashionable cultural stock among children, who bring the current jingles and their variations into the playground. Advertising slogans also frequently test the limits of syntax and semantics, playing with puns and other ambiguities. One car manufacturer's recent campaign exploited the ambiguity of the double negative by advertising a '0% finance' deal with the slogan 'Don't say we never give you nothing'. Advertising texts range around the visual potential of different kinds of writing, from enormous letters on hoardings to those which the reader has to strain to see.

As texts for children to investigate and compose themselves, advertisements offer opportunities at a number of levels. The choice of individual words (LX), such as product names, is important, and encourages children to think about the effect of the sounds of words (P/O) and the link between these and the semantic connotations (S). To make a successful advertisement, children will need to think about the best genre for the kind of product in question. In Sealey (1990) I described how some children in Years 5 and 6 chose the name *Unicorn* for an imaginary chocolate bar, and then made up a short script in a fairy-tale genre as a television commercial for it. The constraints and conventions of the medium led them to concentrate on details such as rephrasing the slogan from 'Grab one [a Unicorn bar] and you'll have your wish' to 'Catch a Unicorn and he'll grant your wish'. The children described the first version as 'too common' and 'too Brummie' and preferred the second because it was 'more magical', adjusting the micro details of lexical choice in relation to the requirements of the discourse in its social context.

Many advertisements make a bid to stay in the memory by using rhyme, and, again, composing an advertisement creates a context for experimenting with rhyme and other poetic devices such as alliteration (the repetition of initial sounds) and assonance (the repetition of similar vowel sounds in the stressed syllables of neighbouring words, as in *sweet dreams* (P/O)).

Crinson (1990) describes another context in which rhymes were the texts through which children in Year 6 learned more about stressed and unstressed syllables, tone groups and verse patterns (P/O). His starting point was the rhymes which children use in the playground, including the choosing rhymes used to determine who is to be 'it' in games, and rhymes to accompany skipping. The children were introduced to the idea of heavy and light syllables, learning the notation and marking their own names accordingly. They recited rhymes like 'Humpty Dumpty' and compared the stress used to make such 'binary verse' (as it is technically known) fit rhythmic patterns with the tone groups found in everyday speech. The children made up new choosing rhymes of their own, and might have gone on, had time allowed, to look at other rhythmic verse forms such as rap and dub poems, and the effect in speech of different intonation patterns, or their absence. (How do we respond to the Dalek-like voices which relay telephone numbers from Directory Enquiries, and what exactly tells us that they are different from typical speech?)

Haynes (1992) describes work using rap poems, with the structure of the text giving it predictability and providing a context for another approach to differentiating between content and function words: the stress always falls on the former (G). Teachers can support children with this kind of text, as was suggested above, by supplying parts of the framework, such as the rhyming pairs of words which must come at the end of the lines, leaving them free to compose rhythmic sections to lead up to the rhymes.

The differences between poems and advertisements are more apparent if they are considered from the point of view not of form but of their social significance and status as cultural artefacts (LS). I should not want to suggest that there is nothing more to learn about poetry than the skeleton of verse forms, but older children might find it interesting to debate the respective merits of high and popular culture. Both kinds of text seek to maximize the potential of individual words, often drawing on literary connotations and devices, making the audience work to extract meanings from the text while persuading them to particular points of view. (For a further discussion of these parallels, see Cook, 1992.) You might want to discuss with children whether or not the differences between the advertisement, with its profit motive, and the poem, born of a different kind of human endeavour (at least in contemporary society), outweigh the similarities.

Planning, schemes of work and assessment

It will be obvious that the suggestions included in this chapter do not in themselves constitute a complete and sequenced syllabus for teaching about language. This is partly because the programmes of study included in the National Curriculum for English will inevitably provide the basis for the detailed planning of most teaching, but also because it is impossible to prescribe appropriate teaching content for every situation. What I hope will be useful, however, is to combine suggestions made in the previous chapter, on principles and methods, with some of the teaching suggestions made here, and to work with colleagues to devise schemes of work which take account of both without slavishly following either. Everything which has been suggested as a means of teaching children more *about* language should be consistent with your obligations under the National Curriculum to teach the programmes of study for Speaking and Listening, Reading and Writing.

Some topics identified in the school's overall planning as central themes for a term's or half-term's work will obviously lend themselves to certain aspects of language teaching more readily than others. For example in general terms, a topic-based scheme of work with a science or technology emphasis will probably offer opportunities for exploring aspects of non-narrative discourses, genres and texts, while a topic which draws more on the humanities curriculum may link better with narrative texts and figurative uses of language. Sometimes your topic may have a very definite language focus, while at other times the teaching about language will be less central, and integrated into other curriculum areas.

The checklist which was provided at the end of the previous chapter can be adapted to ensure coverage of the various aspects of language study outlined in this chapter, and Figure 2.1 is a useful tool for ensuring that the different areas of language study will be addressed over a reasonable timescale, such as an academic year. Teachers often find it helpful to adopt the habit of considering at the planning stages of every scheme of work the texts which it will involve. These texts will include the whole range of resources which the children will encounter as reading and reference material, as well as spoken texts which they will view or listen to, and the texts which they will produce as speakers and writers. By sorting these lists in conjunction with your regular auditing of range in the children's experiences of language you will be alerted to the possibilities for teaching about language in the context of your curriculum planning.

On the whole, the National Curriculum at Key Stages 1 and 2 still concentrates on language and literacy *performance* as the focus of assessment rather than seeking to test *knowledge* about language separately and explicitly. The assessment of pupils' achievements in reading, writing, speaking and listening, according to the criteria outlined in the 1995 Order, involves evidence of what children *do*, but it also requires you to monitor their 'awareness' and 'understanding' of various aspects of spoken and written language.

The issues raised in Chapter 3, relating to progression, will need to be addressed with colleagues teaching other age groups, because it is obviously important to avoid repeating some language-teaching content and omitting other aspects, although it is equally important to revisit the basic themes and build on what children have already learned at a more basic level. The axes of progression outlined in Chapter 3 are useful for focusing on and assessing development over a period of time. Relevant questions are: Has the child's experience of spoken and written language increased? Has the child encountered and produced a wider range of types of text? Is the child able to make more precise and sophisticated observations about various examples of spoken and written language than before? How far can the child abstract and generalize about the aspects of language and literacy associated with the level achieved in each of the attainment targets, and is this ability greater than it was?

Conclusion

This chapter has illustrated some of the ways in which texts can be used as the central resource for teaching children about language. Texts about language itself, for children both to read and to produce for themselves, are an obvious group of text types. Individual words can be explored in context, using games and riddles, among other things. Both narrative and non-chronological texts can be explored in terms of their structure. Language varieties, both geographical and historical, can be a focus of study, without overlooking the cultural and social significance of variety in the language used among different groups of people. There are various ways in which explorations of syntax can be integrated into a textual approach to teaching about language, and some of them have been explored in this chapter. Language study should ideally be engaging and fun, and the potential of language games for increasing children's linguistic knowledge has also been raised here. Two particular kinds of text have been suggested as especially fruitful for teaching about language, namely poems and advertisements. The chapter has not offered a rigid prescription for planning teaching about language, but has suggested that the principles identified in the previous chapter, combined with the more detailed ideas presented here, may be used as a kind of checklist for planning schemes of work, taking the texts to be used in all curriculum areas as the initial resource around which to plan. Taken in conjunction with the axes of progression in learning about language which were presented in Chapter 3, the approach to planning presented in this chapter also offers pointers to use in the process of assessment.

I hope you will find that you can adapt and develop the suggestions given in this chapter so that your pupils' awareness and understanding of a wide range of the characteristics of spoken and written language are developed, at both micro and macro levels. The concluding chapter summarizes the approaches which have been presented in the book and highlights the issues it has raised for teachers teaching and children learning about language.

Conclusion

This chapter aims to consolidate the main issues which have been addressed in earlier chapters of the book, to provide busy teachers with a concise summary of some of the important points. In this sense, it is intended as a kind of checklist for quick reference, but I should not have written the rest of the book if I thought that the issues could satisfactorily be encapsulated in 'bullet-point' form. You should relate the items included here to the more extensive discussions in the preceding chapters. The order of the items does not follow exactly the sequence of the preceding chapters, since the themes listed here have been discussed at various points throughout the book.

The context

- Any contemporary teaching about language as part of an English curriculum occurs in the context of controversy about how language is best described, why children need to learn about it, and what they need to know.
- These differences of belief and policy are not new, and we may be sure that we have not heard – or read – the last words on the subject.

Ways of describing language

- Language has traditionally been studied in relation to the elements of which it is composed. These microlinguistic categories are useful for description and analysis, but they do not necessarily reflect the ways in which we learn to use a language or the ways in which we learn about language.
- Language can also be considered at a macro level. It is a social practice, bound up with individual and group identities, and linked to social structures and relationships.
- Teaching about language needs to take account of both microlinguistic features and macrolinguistic contexts and functions. Children do not progress from understanding one to learning about the other, but learn increasingly more about both these aspects.

- A key characteristic of language is its variety. Language varies across a number of dimensions. These include: times; places; forms and genres; modes (speech and writing); audiences/participants and the relationships between them; purposes and functions; contexts; content; and media (paper, video-tape, audio-tape, computer screen).

Explicit knowledge about language

- Children's facility with their first language, especially in its spoken forms, is linked with their *implicit* knowledge about language.
- A general aim in teaching about language is to encourage children to become more *explicitly* aware of language as a crucial medium of communication. Bringing language itself into focus is the aim of language awareness and consciousness raising.
- 'Critical language awareness' acknowledges that there are many aspects of language in social relationships which are contested, and it emphasizes learners' active role in making decisions about their own and others' language choices.
- Learning to be literate may be a critical phase in the development of metalinguistic awareness.
- Working on the collaborative drafting of a text can bring features of language to children's conscious attention, especially:
  - when planning what the text will be like;
  - when reviewing progress;
  - at times of uncertainty, disagreement, ambiguity.
- Contrasting the features of different texts also brings language to listeners'/readers' conscious attention.

Using texts to teach about language

- Teaching about language can be planned to maximize opportunities for investigating texts as examples of naturally occurring language.
- Opportunities for children to learn about language occur across the curriculum, because texts are generated in all subjects.
- Teachers can keep their own checklists, ensuring that children do encounter texts which will develop their knowledge about language. Such texts will embody diversity across a range of dimensions, as listed above.
- The National Curriculum divisions of English into 'speaking and listening', 'reading' and 'writing' may not be helpful for planning teaching about language, which can arise as children:
  - move between the different modes, working collaboratively, through talk;
  - learn to empathize with readers when writing;
  - compare and contrast the differences in texts which vary across the dimensions listed above, including comparing spoken language with writing.

- Texts can be used to teach children about language as they:

  - use texts produced by others as models for their own text productions;
  - learn to regard texts as evidence of what language can be like, as data for investigation;
  - look for patterns in language 'data', hypothesize about language and generate 'rules' for themselves;
  - produce texts for authentic, or simulated, purposes and audiences.

- Teaching about language can arise from work such as the following:

  - producing texts about language (dictionaries, alphabet books or friezes, books of word puzzles, riddles, codes, jokes, puns, tongue twisters, and so on);
  - research into the origins of words, spelling patterns, word families, names, and so on, with children displaying their findings;
  - collecting and analysing texts (spoken and written) with particular properties, such as texts consisting of one word or phrase;
  - investigating the structures of different kinds of texts by cutting them up, reassembling them, identifying connectives, sequencing devices, identity 'chains' including pronouns;
  - using the computer to manipulate texts in different ways;
  - using drama and role play, audio-tape and video-tape to generate spoken texts whose structure can be analysed in various ways;
  - surveys into the linguistic diversity in the school and community, including information about accent, dialect, regional and national languages, oral fluency and written scripts;
  - investigations into changes in language over time, using old texts of various kinds (dated children's stories, extracts from Shakespeare, 'classic' poetry, letters and diaries from local studies collections, older and contemporary television programmes, and so on);
  - experimenting with grouping words in sentences by their function and form, and generating 'rules' about how these patterns work;
  - teachers capitalizing on incidental opportunities to point out grammatical features of texts encountered in other teaching contexts;
  - teachers capitalizing on situations where spoken and written language about the same topic can be compared and contrasted;
  - using poems and advertisements to explore the potential and limits of language to communicate a lot in a constrained form, and to consider rhyme, rhythm, alliteration, metaphor, and so on.

Pedagogical issues

- Children can learn a lot about language by investigation. They can generate 'rules' and consider how to display the things they find out. They can learn about how they learn best, and how to generalize from the particular.
- However, children will not 'discover' all there is to know about language

merely by investigating texts. Teachers need both to structure and facilitate investigations, and to recognize when specific information will best be understood by direct instruction.

- Some kinds of language use are specific to classrooms. The small-group talk generated by students collaborating to solve a task, or the writing exercise in which a new piece of learning is explicated or consolidated, are examples of classroom-specific discourses.
- Classroom-specific language is authentic in its own way and teachers need have no fear of explicit teaching based on pedagogic principles in which they have confidence.

Resources for teaching about language

- The principle resources which teachers need to accumulate to support successful teaching about language are texts of as wide a variety as possible. It is helpful to acquire a habit of listening and looking out for examples of language in current use which illustrate specific features. Your collection might include, in addition to the many kinds of books, poems and other classroom texts available anyway:
  - greetings cards;
  - 'junk' mail (especially if aimed at children, directly or via their parents);
  - taped commercials from television and radio, and other short taped media material, especially from local radio in programmes where regional features are relevant, sometimes with transcripts, if possible (beware of copyright regulations);
  - pamphlets, leaflets and other promotional texts, especially if related to places or things significant to children;
  - comics, newspapers and magazines;
  - packages and labels;
  - letters (and envelopes), postcards;
  - texts in a variety of languages;
  - texts produced in earlier times.
- Look out as well for texts *about* language. These include:
  - letters to the press;
  - word games and puzzles;
  - dictionaries of all kinds;
  - old texts about language (textbooks, exercise books, dictionaries, old reading primers).

Progression and assessment in learning about language

- Actual language in use is collaborative and dialogic, yet there is a requirement to regard pupils as isolated individuals for the purposes of assessment and reporting.

- The 1995 English National Curriculum is more geared to the assessment of children's skills and abilities in language *competence* (as talkers, readers and writers) than to assessing their *explicit knowledge* about language.
- Progression in children's knowledge about language is marked by:
  - increasing experience of engaging with, and attending to, language (texts, genres, discourses);
  - increasing precision and sophistication in identifying features of language across various dimensions;
  - the ability to make these observations with an increasing degree of abstraction, to appreciate generalities of which specific instances may be examples.

Above all, learning about language is interesting and rewarding. There are always new texts to investigate, new ideas to apply, new comparisons to be made. Teachers and children can go on together finding out more about the dynamic, human, social phenomenon which is real language.

Glossary

clause A unit of grammatical organization larger than the word or phrase; a 'main' clause may be a sentence in its own right (although it can be joined to other clauses within a sentence) but a 'subordinate' clause cannot stand alone and form a complete sentence. Thus, *a cup of tea* is a phrase. *She poured a cup of tea* is a main clause and could be a sentence. *When she had poured a cup of tea* is a subordinate clause, which needs a main clause to make a complete sentence, such as *When she had poured a cup of tea, she chose a biscuit from the tin.*

content words See open/closed classes of words.

discourse Spoken or written language as it occurs in social and cultural contexts. The conception of language as discourse takes account of the idea that it is a form of social practice, linked with social structures and relationships, and that the ways in which people use it vary accordingly.

function words See open/closed classes of words.

genres Particular *types* of oral or written communication into which texts may be classified, using considerations of structure, form and purpose. Examples would include recipes, sports commentaries (oral) and reports (written), fairy tales, doctor–patient interviews, and so on. The various categories are rarely 'watertight', however.

grammatical words See open/closed classes of words.

grapho-phonic correspondence The relationship between written symbols and the sounds of a language; see sound–symbol relationships.

inflect/inflection See morphology.

lexical words See open/closed classes of words.

lexis The words of a language, its vocabulary.

macrolinguistic See microlinguistic.

metalanguage Language for referring to language itself; 'metalinguistic awareness' is awareness of language as a medium of communication.

microlinguistic Refers to the smaller elements of language, such as sounds, morphemes (see morphology) and words, singly and in combination, up to the level of the sentence; contrasts with 'macrolinguistic', which refers to concerns about longer stretches of language in social contexts.

morphology The study of the forms of words, focusing on how morphemes, the smallest units of meaning, are combined in words. Prefixes such as *un-* and *dis-*, and suffixes such as *-ness* and *-ment*, can be added to free morphemes, which can occur as separate words; hence *un-happi-ness* and *dis-engage-ment*. The addition of a morpheme can 'inflect' a word, altering it from singular to plural (by means of the inflection *-s*), or from present to past tense (*-ed*), for example.

nominalization Occurs when a noun or noun phrase is formed from a word of another class. For example, a child's simulated newspaper article contains the information that *pollution causes algae growth*, rather than saying that *pollution causes algae to grow*. Such constructions are more prevalent in written English than in its spoken mode.

open/closed classes of words A way of distinguishing between classes of words such as nouns and adjectives, to which new items are frequently added ('open' classes), and those such as pronouns, prepositions and conjunctions, to which new items are not normally added ('closed' classes). The terms 'content' (as opposed to 'function') words and 'lexical' (as opposed to 'grammatical') words convey a similar kind of distinction. Thus, words such as *table, huge, worry* have propositional content, whereas words such as *the, with, if* do not on their own have propositional content.

orthography Concerned with representing the sounds of the language in writing; spelling.

paralinguistics Features of spoken language which are non-verbal, such as sighs; some authorities include facial expressions and gestures.

phonology The study of the range and function of sounds in specific languages.

phrase See clause.

pragmatics The semantics of utterances; the meanings created by speakers and listeners in interpersonal contexts.

prefix See morphology.

prosody Systematic variations in the pitch, loudness, tempo and rhythm of spoken language.

semantics The relationship between language and meaning.

sound–symbol relationships There is a correspondence between written language and speech insofar as the symbols used in writing (letters) bear a relationship to the sounds of the language; phonic approaches to reading and writing make extensive use of this correspondence.

suffix See morphology.

syntax The branch of grammar which is concerned with the way words are combined to form phrases, clauses and sentences.

text A complete stretch of language in either speech or writing (although speech is usually transcribed into writing when it is to be considered as a 'text').

word classes Words may be divided according to their formal, functional and semantic properties into groups such as nouns, verbs, prepositions, and so on. These were traditionally referred to as 'parts of speech', but are now more frequently described as 'word classes'.

References

Ahlberg, J. and Ahlberg, A. (1986) *The Jolly Postman, or Other People's Letters*, London: Heinemann.

Aitchison, J. (1991) *Language Change: Progress or Decay?*, 2nd edn, Cambridge: Cambridge University Press.

Bakhtin, M.M. (1981) *The Dialogic Imagination: Four Essays by M.M. Bakhtin*, M. Holquist (ed.), C. Emerson and M. Holquist (trans.), Austin: University of Texas Press.

Ball, S., Kenny, A. and Gardiner, D. (1990) Literacy, politics and the teaching of English. In I. Goodson and P. Medway (eds) *Bringing English to Order*, Lewes: Falmer Press.

Ballance, D. and Ballance, H. (1979) *Nelson Grammar*, Books 1–4, Walton-on-Thames: Thomas Nelson and Sons.

Barnes, D. (1986) Language in the secondary classroom. In D. Barnes, J. Britton and M. Torbe (eds) *Language, the Learner and the School*, 3rd edn, Harmondsworth: Penguin.

Bartlett, R. and Fogg, D. (1992) Language in the environment. In R. Bain, B. Fitzgerald and M. Taylor (eds) *Looking into Language: Classroom Approaches to Knowledge About Language*, Sevenoaks: Hodder and Stoughton.

Barton, D. (1994) *Literacy: An Introduction to the Ecology of Written Language*, Oxford: Blackwell.

Bawden, N. (1975) *The Peppermint Pig*, London: Victor Gollancz.

Berthoud-Papandropoulou, I. (1978) An experimental study of children's ideas about language. In A. Sinclair, R.J. Jarvella and W.J.M. Levelt (eds) *The Child's Conception of Language*, Berlin: Springer-Verlag.

Blank, M. and Solomon, F. (1972) How shall the disadvantaged child be taught? In Language and Learning Course Team at the Open University, *Language in Education: A Source Book*, London: Routledge and Kegan Paul.

Board of Education (1921) *The Teaching of English in England* (The Newbolt Report), London: HMSO.

Board of Education (1931) *Report of the Consultative Committee on the Primary School* (The Hadow Report), London: HMSO.

Bolinger, D. (1980) *Language: The Loaded Weapon*, Harlow: Longman.

Bolton, W.F. (ed.) (1966) *The English Language: Essays by English and American Men of Letters*, Cambridge: Cambridge University Press.

Bowey, J.A. and Tunmer, W.E. (1984) Word awareness in children. In W.E. Tunmer, C. Pratt and M.L. Herriman (eds) *Metalinguistic Awareness in Children*, Berlin: Springer-Verlag.

Brown, P. and Levinson, S. (1978) Universals in language usage. In E.N. Goody (ed.) *Questions and Politeness: Strategies in Social Interaction*, Cambridge: Cambridge University Press.

Bruner, J. (1985) Vygotsky: a historical and conceptual perspective. In J.V. Wertsch (ed.) *Culture, Communication and Cognition: Vygotskian Perspectives*, Cambridge: Cambridge University Press.

Bruner, J. (1986) *Actual Minds, Possible Worlds*, Cambridge, Mass.: Harvard University Press.

Burgess, C., Burgess, T., Cartland, L., Chambers, R., Hedgeland, J., Levine, N., Mole, J., Newsome, B., Smith, H. and Torbe, M. (1973) *Understanding Children's Writing*, Harmondsworth: Penguin.

Calfee, R.C., Lindamood, P. and Lindamood, C. (1973) Acoustic-phonetic skills and reading – kindergarten through twelfth grade. In *Journal of Educational Psychology*, Vol. 64, pp. 293–8.

Carter, B. and Burgess, H. (1993) Testing, regulation and control: shifting education narratives. In *Curriculum Studies*, Vol. 1, No. 2, pp. 233–44.

Carter, R. (1990) The new grammar teaching. In R. Carter (ed.) *Knowledge About Language and the Curriculum: The LINC Reader*, Sevenoaks: Hodder and Stoughton.

Central Advisory Council for Education (1967) *Children and their Primary Schools* (The Plowden Report), London: HMSO.

Cherrington, V. (1987) 'Non-narrative writing in the primary school', unpublished B Phil (Ed.) dissertation, University of Birmingham.

Cheshire, J. and Edwards, V. (1993) Sociolinguistics in the classroom. In J. Milroy and L. Milroy (eds) *Real English: The Grammar of English Dialects in the British Isles*, Harlow: Longman.

Chomsky, N. (1988) *Language and Problems of Knowledge*, Cambridge, Mass.: Massachusetts Institute of Technology.

Clark, E.V. (1978) Awareness of language: some evidence from what children say and do. In A. Sinclair, R.J. Jarvella and W.J.M. Levelt (eds) *The Child's Conception of Language*, Berlin: Springer-Verlag.

Clarke, S. (1991) Language snapshots: LINC work in progress. In Southwest Language Project, *Strong Language*, Issue 3, Autumn.

Clarkson, G. and Stansfield, H. (1992) Writing recipes. In R. Bain, B. Fitzgerald and M. Taylor (eds) *Looking into Language: Classroom Approaches to Knowledge About Language*, Sevenoaks: Hodder and Stoughton.

Clymer, T. and Martin, P.M. (1978) *The City*, Aylesbury: Ginn.

Coates, J. (1993) *Women, Men and Language*, 2nd edn, Harlow: Longman.

Cook, G. (1992) *The Discourse of Advertising*, London: Routledge.

Coulthard, M. (1977) *An Introduction to Discourse Analysis*, Harlow: Longman.

Cox, B. (1991) *Cox on Cox: An English Curriculum for the 1990s*, Sevenoaks: Hodder and Stoughton.

Crinson, J. (1990) Rhymes and catches. In *English North*, Northern LINC consortium newsletter No. 2.

Crowley, T. (1989) *The Politics of Discourse: The Standard Language Question in British Cultural Debates*, London: Macmillan.

132 LEARNING ABOUT LANGUAGE

Crystal, D. (1987) *The Cambridge Encyclopedia of Language*, Cambridge: Cambridge University Press.
Crystal, D. (1988) *Rediscover Grammar*, Harlow: Longman.
Dahl, R. (1982) *The BFG*, London: Heinemann.
Davies, B. (1983) The role pupils play in the social construction of classroom order. In *British Journal of Sociology of Education*, Vol. 4, No. 1, pp. 55–69.
Davies, B. and Harré, R. (1991) Positioning: the discursive production of selves. In *Journal for the Theory of Social Behaviour*, Vol. 20, No. 1, pp. 43–63.
Dearing, Sir Ronald (1994) *The National Curriculum and its Assessment, Final Report*, London: SCAA (School Curriculum and Assessment Authority).
DES (Department of Education and Science) (1975) *A Language for Life* (The Bullock Report), London: HMSO.
DES (Department of Education and Science) (1986) *English from 5 to 16*, 2nd edn, incorporating responses – 1st edn 1984, London: HMSO.
DES (Department of Education and Science) (1987) *National Curriculum Task Group on Assessment and Testing: A Report*, London: DES.
DES (Department of Education and Science) (1988a) *Report of the Committee of Inquiry into the Teaching of English Language* (The Kingman Report), London: HMSO.
DES (Department of Education and Science) (1988b) *English for Ages 5 to 11* (The Cox Report), London: HMSO.
DES (Department of Education and Science) (1989) *English for Ages 5 to 16* (The 2nd Cox Report), London: HMSO.
DES (Department of Education and Science) (1991) *How is Your Child Doing at School? A Parent's Guide to Testing*, London: HMSO.
DFE (Department for Education) (1993) *English for Ages 5 to 16 (1993)*, London: HMSO.
DFE (Department for Education) (1995) *English in the National Curriculum*, London: HMSO.
Donaldson, M. (1978) *Children's Minds*, London: Fontana.
Edwards, D. and Mercer, N. (1987) *Common Knowledge: The Development of Understanding in the Classroom*, London: Routledge.
Ellis, R. (1992) *Second Language Acquisition and Language Pedagogy*, Clevedon: Multilingual Matters.
Fairclough, N. (ed.) (1992) *Critical Language Awareness*, London: Longman.
Garton, A. and Pratt, C. (1989) *Learning to be Literate*, Oxford: Basil Blackwell.
Gibson, H. (1992) Beyond a joke: children, humour and knowledge about language. In *English in Education*, Vol. 26, No. 2, Summer, pp. 54–60.
Goffman, E. (1959) *The Presentation of Self in Everyday Life*, New York: Anchor Books.
Gombert, J.E. (1992) *Metalinguistic Development*, Hemel Hempstead: Harvester Wheatsheaf.
Halliday, M.A.K. (1982) Relevant models of language. In B. Wade (ed.) *Language Perspectives*, London: Heinemann.
Halliday, M.A.K. (1989) *Spoken and Written Language*, 2nd edn, Oxford: Oxford University Press.
Harriott, M. (1990) Knowledge about language with particular reference to tense. Unpublished account, LINC project.
Harris, J. (1993) The grammar of Irish English. In J. Milroy and L. Milroy (eds) *Real English: The Grammar of English Dialects in the British Isles*, Harlow: Longman.

Haynes, J. (1992) *A Sense of Words: Knowledge About Language in the Primary School*, Sevenoaks: Hodder and Stoughton.

Hughes, G. A. and Trudgill, P (1987) *English Accents and Dialects: An Introduction to Social and Regional Varieties of English*, London: Edward Arnold.

Hymas, C. (1991) Ministers veto 'wacky' teaching guide. In *Sunday Times*, 23 June.

Ivanic, R. (1990) Critical language awareness in action. In R. Carter (ed.) *Knowledge About Language and the Curriculum: The LINC Reader*, Sevenoaks: Hodder and Stoughton.

Johnson, R. (1991) A new road to serfdom? A critical history of the 1988 Act. In Department of Cultural Studies (ed.) *Education Limited: Schooling, Training and the New Right in England since 1979*, London: Unwin Hyman.

Keith, G. (unpublished paper) 'Knowledge about language: an investigative approach for teachers and pupils', LINC Project.

Labov, W. (1972) *Language in the Inner City*, Oxford: Basil Blackwell.

Lee, D. (1992) *Competing Discourses*, Harlow: Longman.

Leech, G., Deuchar, M. and Hoogenraad, R. (1982) *English Grammar for Today*, London: Macmillan.

Martin, J. (1989) *Factual Writing: Exploring and Challenging Social Reality*, 2nd edn, Oxford: Oxford University Press.

Mason, J. (1991) The writing of narrative, chronological and information texts. In Gloucestershire LINC project, *Breaking New Ground*, Gloucester: Gloucestershire County Council.

Massey, R. (1991) In *Daily Mail*, 26 June.

Maybin, J. (1994) Children's voices: talk, knowledge and identity. In D. Graddol, J. Maybin and B. Stierer (eds) *Researching Language and Literacy in Social Context*, Clevedon: Multilingual Matters.

McCarthy, M. and Carter, R. (1994) *Language as Discourse: Perspectives for Language Teaching*, Harlow: Longman.

Meighan, R. (1986) *A Sociology of Educating*, 2nd edn, London: Cassell.

Milroy, J. and Milroy, L. (eds) (1993) *Real English: The Grammar of English Dialects in the British Isles*, Harlow: Longman.

Milroy, L. (1984) Comprehension and context: successful communication and communication breakdown. In P. Trudgill (ed.) *Applied Sociolinguistics*, London: Academic Press Inc.

Nunan, D. (1993) *Introducing Discourse Analysis*, London: Penguin.

Ottaway, A.K.C. (1953) *Education and Society*, London: Routledge and Kegan Paul.

Perec, G. (1988) *Life, A User's Manual*, London: Collins Harvill.

Perera, K. (1982a) The assessment of linguistic difficulty in reading material. In R. Carter (ed.) *Linguistics and the Teacher*, London: Routledge and Kegan Paul.

Perera, K. (1982b) The language demands of school learning. In R. Carter (ed.) *Linguistics and the Teacher*, London: Routledge and Kegan Paul.

Perera, K. (1984) *Children's Writing and Reading*, Oxford: Basil Blackwell.

Perera, K. (1990) Grammatical differentiation between speech and writing in children aged 8 to 12. In R. Carter (ed.) *Knowledge About Language and the Curriculum: The LINC Reader*, Sevenoaks: Hodder and Stoughton.

Peters, M. (1985 edition) *Spelling: Caught or Taught?*, London: Routledge.

Quirk, R. and Greenbaum, S. (1973) *A University Grammar of English*, London: Longman.

Quirk, R. and Stein, G. (1990) *English in Use*, Harlow: Longman.

Rawson, K. (1990) The last wilderness: language, power and performance. In Southwest Language Project, *Strong Language*, Issue 1, Summer.

Richmond, J. (1990) What do we mean by knowledge about language? In R. Carter (ed.) *Knowledge About Language and the Curriculum: The LINC Reader*, Sevenoaks: Hodder and Stoughton.

Rogers, C. (1991) Action research in the classroom: investigating language. In Gloucestershire LINC project, *Breaking New Ground*, Gloucester: Gloucestershire County Council.

Rosen, H. (1988) Struck by a particular gap. In A. West and M. Jones (eds) *Learning Me Your Language: Perspectives on the Teaching of English*, Cheltenham: Stanley Thornes.

SCAA (School Curriculum and Assessment Authority) (1994a) *Evaluation of the Implementation of English in the National Curriculum at Key Stages 1, 2 and 3 (1991–1993)*, London: SCAA.

SCAA (School Curriculum and Assessment Authority) (1994b) *English in the National Curriculum: Draft Proposals*, London: SCAA.

Scarry, R. (1980) *Mix or Match Storybook*, London: Collins.

Sealey, A. (1990) Magic words: helping young children to develop their knowledge about language. In R. Carter (ed.) *Knowledge About Language and the Curriculum: The LINC Reader*, Sevenoaks: Hodder and Stoughton.

Sealey, A. (1992) The Dazzlers' Dictionary. In R. Bain, B. Fitzgerald and M. Taylor (eds) *Looking into Language: Classroom Approaches to Knowledge About Language*, Sevenoaks: Hodder and Stoughton.

Sealey, A. (1994) What do they mean? An analysis of one child's language awareness. In *International Journal of Early Childhood*, Vol. 26, No. 1, pp. 33–40.

Showell, R. (1975) *Living Things*, Loughborough: Ladybird.

Sinclair, J. and Coulthard, R. (1975) *Towards an Analysis of Discourse*, Oxford: Oxford University Press.

Slater, L. (1992) Writing newspaper stories. In R. Bain, B. Fitzgerald and M. Taylor (eds) *Looking into Language: Classroom Approaches to Knowledge About Language*, Sevenoaks: Hodder and Stoughton.

Smith, F. (1992) Watch with mother, or view with mum? In R. Bain, B. Fitzgerald and M. Taylor (eds) *Looking into Language: Classroom Approaches to Knowledge About Language*, Sevenoaks: Hodder and Stoughton.

Stratta, L. and Dixon, J. (1992) The National Curriculum in English: does genre theory have anything to offer? In *English in Education*, Vol. 26, No. 2, pp. 16–27.

Swann, J. (1989) Talk control: an illustration from the classroom of problems of analysing male dominance in education. In J. Coates and D. Cameron (eds) *Women in Their Speech Communities*, London: Longman.

Thomas, L. (1993) *Beginning Syntax*, Oxford: Blackwell.

Tizard, B. and Hughes, M. (1984) *Young Children Learning: Talking and Thinking at Home and School*, London: Fontana.

Tizard, B., Hughes, M., Carmichael, H. and Pinkerton, G. (1988) Language and social class: is verbal deprivation a myth? In N. Mercer (ed.) *Language and Literacy from an Educational Perspective*, Vol. 2, Milton Keynes: Open University Press.

Tolkien, J.R.R. (1966 edition) *The Hobbit*, London: Unwin.

Tough, J. (1977) *Talking and Learning: A Guide to Fostering Communication Skills in Nursery and Infant Schools*, London: Ward Lock Educational.

Tunmer, W.E. and Grieve, R. (1984) Syntactic awareness in children. In W.E. Tunmer,

C. Pratt and M.L. Herriman (eds) *Metalinguistic Awareness in Children*, Berlin: Springer-Verlag.

van Lier, L. (1995) *Introducing Language Awareness*, London: Penguin.

Wardaugh, R. (1992) *An Introduction to Sociolinguistics*, 2nd edn, Oxford: Blackwell.

Wells, G. (1987) *The Meaning Makers: Children Learning Language and Using Language to Learn*, 2nd edn, Sevenoaks: Hodder and Stoughton.

West, A. and Jones, M. (1988) Preface. In A. West and M. Jones (eds) *Learning Me Your Language: Perspectives on the Teaching of English*, Cheltenham: Stanley Thornes.

Wilkinson, J. (1995) *Introducing Standard English*, London: Penguin.

Willes, M. (1983) *Children into Pupils: A Study of Language in Early Schooling*, London: Routledge.

Index

DEVELOPING READERS IN THE MIDDLE YEARS

Elaine Millard

Are there developmental stages in reading response? Can these be promoted or accelerated by classroom experience? The debate about standards in reading has largely ignored such questions and focused on the methods used to introduce children to print in the early years of school. Less attention has been given to ways of nurturing the habit once the first stages are past. Elaine Millard explores how assumptions about what is pleasurable in reading set an agenda for the middle years which ignores crucial differences in children's reading habits, particularly those related to gender. She argues that the more advanced reading skills of analysis, evaluation and critical response can be introduced to children at this stage but that they require the support of a classroom context that encourages cooperation and which builds on shared habits of reading.

Contents

176pp   0 335 19071 5 (paperback)

CREATIVE TEACHERS IN PRIMARY SCHOOLS

Peter Woods

Is creative teaching still possible in English schools? Can teachers maintain and promote their own interests and beliefs as well as deliver a prescribed National Curriculum?

This book explores creative teachers' attempts to pursue *their* brand of teaching despite the changes. Peter Woods has discovered a range of strategies and adaptations to this end among such teachers, including resisting change which runs counter to their own values; appropriating the National Curriculum within their own ethos; enhancing their role through the use of others; and enriching their work through the National Curriculum to provide quality learning experiences. If all else fails, such teachers remove themselves from the system and take their creativity elsewhere. A strong theme of self-determination runs through these experiences.

While acknowledging hard realities, the book is ultimately optimistic, and a tribute to the dedication and inspiration of primary teachers.

The book makes an important contribution to educational theory, showing a range of responses to *intensification* as well as providing many detailed examples of collaborative research methods.

Contents

208pp   0 335 19313 7 (paperback)   0 335 19314 5 (hardback)

EDUCATING THE WHOLE CHILD
CROSS-CURRICULAR SKILLS, THEMES AND DIMENSIONS

John and Iram Siraj-Blatchford (eds)

This book approaches the 'delivery' of the cross-curricular skills, themes and dimensions from a perspective emphasizing the culture of primary schools and the social worlds of children. The authors argue that the teaching of skills, attitudes, concepts and knowledge to young children should not be seen as separate or alternative objectives, but rather as complementary and essential elements of the educational process. It is the teacher's role to help children develop and build upon the understandings, skills, knowledge and attitudes which they bring with them into school. Learning for young children is a social activity where new skills and understandings are gained through interaction with both adults and with their peers. Each of the approaches outlined in the book is thus grounded in an essential respect and empathy for children and childhood as a distinct stage in life and not merely a preparation for the world of adulthood. For instance, the authors argue that responsibilities and decision-making are everyday experiences for children and that they need to be able to develop attitudes and skills which enable them to participate fully in their own social world.

Contents
Cross-curricular skills, themes and dimensions: an introduction – Little citizens: helping children to help each other – Effective schooling for all: the 'special educational needs' dimension – Racial equality education: identity, curriculum and pedagogy – 'Girls don't do bricks': gender and sexuality in the primary classroom – Children in an economic world: young children learning in a consumerist and post-industrial society – Catching them young: careers education in the primary years – Understanding environmental education for the primary classroom – Health education in the primary school: back to basics? – The place of PSE in the primary school – Index.

Contributors
John Bennett, Debra Costley, Debbie Epstein, Peter Lang, Val Millman, Lina Patel, Alistair Ross, Ann Sinclair Taylor, Iram Siraj-Blatchford, John Siraj-Blatchford, Balbir Kaur Sohal, Janice Wale.

192pp   0 335 19444 3 (paperback)   0 335 19445 1 (hardback)